Tuned-In Teaching

Dear Readers,

Much like the diet phenomenon Eat This, Not That, this series aims to replace some existing practices with approaches that are more effective—healthier, if you will—for our students. We hope to draw attention to practices that have little support in research or professional wisdom, and to offer alternatives that have greater support. Each text is collaboratively written by authors representing research and practice. Section 1 offers practitioner perspective(s) on a practice in need of replacing and helps us understand the challenges, temptations, and misunderstandings that have led us to this ineffective approach. Section 2 provides researcher perspective(s) on the lack of research to support the ineffective practice(s), and reviews research supporting better approaches. In Section 3, the author(s) representing practitioner perspective(s) give detailed descriptions of how to implement these better practices. By the end of each book, you will understand both what not to do, and what to do, to improve student learning.

It takes courage to question one's own practice—to shift away from what you may have seen throughout your years in education and toward something new that you may have seen few, if any, colleagues use. We applaud you for demonstrating that courage and wish you the very best in your journey from this to that.

Best wishes,
— *M. Colleen Cruz* and *Nell K. Duke, Series Editors*

NOT THIS BUT THAT

Tuned-In Teaching: Centering Youth Culture for an Active and Just Classroom

ANTERO GARCIA AND ERNEST MORRELL

HEINEMANN
PORTSMOUTH, NH

Heinemann
145 Maplewood Avenue, Suite 300
Portsmouth, NH 03801
www.heinemann.com

Offices and agents throughout the world

The authors and publisher wish to thank those who have generously given permission to reprint borrowed material:

Excerpt from "From Digital Consumption to Digital Invention: Toward a New Critical Theory and Practice of Multiliteracies" by Nicole Mirra, Ernest Morrell, and Danielle Filipiak from *Theory Into Practice*, Vol. 57, Issue 1, 22 Jan 2018. Published by Routledge. Reprinted by permission of the Copyright Clearance Center on behalf of Taylor & Francis Ltd, http://www.tandfonline.com.

Excerpt reprinted by permission from the Copyright Clearance Center on behalf of Springer Nature: Springer Nature, *The Urban Review*, Vol. 32, No. 2, Jan 1, 2020, "Constructing Meaning About Violence, School, and Community: Participatory Action Research with Urban Youth" by Alice McIntyre, © 2000 by Human Sciences Press, Inc.

Library of Congress Cataloging-in-Publication Data
Names: Garcia, Antero, author. | Morrell, Ernest, author.
Title: Tuned-in teaching : centering youth culture for an active and just
    classroom / Antero Garcia and Ernest Morrell.
Description: Portsmouth, NH : Heinemann, [2022] | Series: Not this but that
    | Includes bibliographical references.
Identifiers: LCCN 2021057425 | ISBN 9780325136479
Subjects: LCSH: Culturally relevant pedagogy—United States. |
    Student-centered learning—United States. | Teacher-student
    relationships—United States.
Classification: LCC LC1099.515.C85 G37 2022 | DDC
    370.117—dc23/eng/20220125
LC record available at https://lccn.loc.gov/2021057425

Series Editors: Nell K. Duke and M. Colleen Cruz
Editors: Zoë Ryder White and Margaret LaRaia
Production Editor: Kimberlee Sims
Cover and Interior Designer: Monica Ann Cohen
Typesetter: Valerie Levy, Drawing Board Studios
Manufacturing: Val Cooper

Printed in the United States of America on acid-free paper
1 2 3 4 5 MPP 26 25 24 23 22 PO 33997

CONTENTS

INTRODUCTION

M. Colleen Cruz

*I*f you're anything like me, you have a friend or family member, maybe someone in your community, who you talk to when you want someone to "give it to you straight." These are the people who refuse to lie or flatter us and will never gaslight us. For me it's been a small handful of people over the years: my mom, my hairstylist, and Sam, who runs the bodega on my corner to name a few. When I am wrestling with something, when an idea I have or an action I want to take is new and fragile and I just want to ruminate on it, I never talk to them. I know that I should only ask them for their wisdom if I am truly ready to hear what they think. Because they will absolutely tell the truth. But when I have hit the limit of the work I can do on my own, when I suspect I am flattering myself or simply know I need a fresh perspective, I reach out to them.

"Hey, Sam. One coffee, regular. One egg and cheese. And one question—do you think I can come off as cold sometimes? Or do people know I'm an introvert?"

As Sam slides my coffee over, he gives me the look, "OK. I have a lot to say about this . . ." Agree or not with what Sam and other truth-tellers say, we know that we can't go back to *not* knowing. Once we find the answers, we can't unknow.

The text you are about to read is the book version of that person. I suspect that if you are holding this book, it's because you feel an itch, a curiosity, perhaps even a sneaking suspicion, that your teaching could be more tuned in and that you could be more connected to your students and their needs and ways of learning in this world. Whether this is a new(ish) area of study, begun during pandemic teaching, or something that has been developing for years, matters less than that you have met-aphorically shown up at the bodega, ready for Ernest Morrell and Antero Garcia to give it to you straight.

Teaching and learning theory, research and demands, although never static, have been developing at warp speed. Combine that with the steady hum of cultural shift, youth voice amplification, and digital media outreach, and even the most up-to-date, of-the-moment, connected pedagogue is bound to feel a bit less sure-footed. In this book, Ernest and Antero slide over the coffee and the rest of the goods. They name the obstacles to authentic connection teachers face every day, and they let us know that weird disconnected feeling is not entirely our fault (yet). As they take us through the decades of research and scholarship, they show us that much of what might feel disparate at first glance (What do studies on critical literacies have in common with mathematics, let alone youth participatory action research projects?) is connected in deep and compelling ways. Antero and Ernest then look us straight in the eye and let us know exactly how we can tune in to our students. Not through gimmicks or awkward attempts at being the cool teacher, but through actionable steps that will never go out of style.

NOT THIS 🚦 BUT THAT

Tuned-In Teaching: Centering Youth Culture for an Active and Just Classroom

SECTION **1**

NOT ● **THIS**

*Out-of-Touch
Teaching: Its
Accidental Origins*

ANTERO GARCIA AND ERNEST MORRELL

Consider, for a moment, the incredible energy that courses through the veins of your classroom each day. From the vibrant energy of students converging with enthusiasm on the ideas and challenges you pose to them, to the authentic audiences they speak to via the work they produce, to the transformative texts that students scrutinize, ours are classrooms of possibilities and hope. Sure, your day-to-day teaching life may not always sing in harmony with these exact possibilities all the time, but you, certainly, have felt what it is like when your classroom comes to life and you, your students, and your curriculum resonate and live *in the moment* of learning and connection.

We begin this book with a recognition that these moments are *never* permanent. Memorable classroom experiences exist because they stand in contrast to what the rest of school deems as ordinary. So, let's agree on a couple caveats about the limits of your classroom instruction:

1. There is no such thing as a perfect classroom, only the pedagogical boundaries that you and your students build and traverse together.

2. You will make mistakes in your teaching career. Embrace these as gifts from which you and your students will grow.

Because our classrooms ebb and flow with the various degrees of what can happen in any given moment, our capacity to shift and sway with the demands of the present is perhaps one of the most fundamental and least supported aspects of our profession. Furthermore, our classrooms sway, rock, and jostle with the nature of the world. If our classrooms are disrupted or moved online as a result of

Our classrooms sway, rock, and jostle with the nature of the world.

a global pandemic (as a contemporary example) or are feeling the sting of a local injustice or activist issue shaping your school community, these are phenomena that cannot be walled off from the classroom. Whether we bring them up or not, these are topics that are here and as present in the minds of our students as the texts in front of them or, worse, the abstract essay topics and standardized tests they may be asked to take.

As we consider some of the ways in which we can understand our role as teachers, let's also consider the ways that students play an integral role in transforming a classroom into a space for radical innovation. As a collective, teachers and students can have aligned goals for action, engagement, and joy in our shared learning journey. This is a process of ensuring that we, as teachers, are working in solidarity with our community of learners. It is a humbling, rewarding task. It is also not always an easy one.

As we consider some of the ways in which we can understand our role as teachers, let's also consider the ways that students play an integral role in transforming a classroom into a space for radical innovation.

Despite all these exciting possibilities, sometimes our classrooms can feel *stuck*. The rut you feel might come from a sense of doing the same thing day in and day out. It might come from students who don't seem as excited when engaging with the curriculum as they might be. The rut might even come from a creeping sense that what and how you are teaching feel further disconnected from the rapidly shifting world beyond the walls of your classroom. Particularly as they naturally progress through adolescent growth and prepare for the wondrous world that they will change beyond school, young people's lives are complex. Importantly, our world is also one that is always changing.

At some point in your career, this feeling of "stuckness" will creep into the corners and crevices of your classroom. Maybe you're feeling a sense of sameness: you're teaching the same texts in the same ways with the same tools year in and year out. Maybe you're feeling stuck, on the other hand, because of the sheer amount of change happening around you: the constant ebb and flow of administrative oversight that purports to know what you and your students need rather than relying on your expertise as the teacher. Maybe you're just plain tired. The physical, intellectual, and emotional labor of teaching is profound, and the world of professional development does not always treat teachers with the dignity and respect that must be afforded to one of our most important professions. These, and whatever other reasons you might feel stuck, are all valid. We are writing this in the hopes of supporting your journey to moving back in touch with your pedagogy, with your students, with your discipline, and with yourself. Many different reasons may be to blame, and we're here to focus on transformation and to offer a vocabulary for moving beyond out-of-touch teaching.

The physical, intellectual, and emotional labor of teaching is profound, and the world of professional development does not always treat teachers with the dignity and respect that must be afforded to one of our most important professions.

Naming What We Need to Change in a Changing World

Although the feelings of uncertainty, joy, passion, love, anger, and curiosity of today's students may mirror the same feelings that you once felt sitting in similar desks in similar classrooms in the past, the world that students are learning and interacting in is substantially different.

One concept we have explored with our own students through lessons of critical literacy is the need to *name* ideas, places, and acts around us. Naming is a powerful, liberatory act (Freire and Macedo 1987). In the spirit of this process, we specifically label what we mean when we refer to out-of-touch teaching throughout this book. *Out-of-touch teaching refers*

See Section 3 for a variety of practical strategies for tuned-in, connected teaching.

to pedagogical choices, interactions with students, and instructional materials that do not make an immediate impact on the lives of students, that do not actively work to transform the social conditions of schooling, or that are disconnected from the interests and expertise of contemporary students in the present world. In the context of middle and high school classrooms, such approaches proliferate in many different aspects of instruction. Though we offer multiple strategies throughout this volume, we draw your instructional consideration to a few specific aspects of your teaching:

- The text and curricular selections in your classroom— Who writes the texts that students interact with? When were they produced? In what kinds of modalities and languages?

- The modes of writing and communication that are taught—Who are the implied and explicit audiences for student writing? What modes do students write in? Who provides feedback?

- Relationships with students—What efforts do you make to get to know your students? What biases might you be exhibiting?

- Your own (shifting) interests as a teacher—Is your curriculum at all reflecting the ideas, topics, and content that you've been interested in? Do you give yourself space to breathe and grow in your work?

- The world beyond your classroom—How does your classroom open up or disregard the sociopolitical, emotional, geographic, digital, and *analog* world beyond your school? What policies, assumptions, and material constraints limit this engagement with the world?

As we discuss the research and suggest possibilities for addressing each of these aspects in the remainder of this book, we discuss *how* out-of-touch teaching happens.

Despite the implied idea that we just naturally slide out of touch in our practice, there are important reasons why your teaching might be out of touch. Furthermore, we want you to know it's not your fault! As we work on improving our practice—both collectively and individually—we do so recognizing that there are substantial factors inhibiting the teaching profession and the act of teaching joyfully. This book is not about letting these factors off the hook. Dwindling school funding, an overemphasis on assessment, the stratification of learning opportunities based on socioeconomic difference: the reasons that teachers struggle are profound and adversely affect the learning (and life) outcomes of young people, particularly students from Black, indigenous, and nondominant communities. We go into these factors next, and we note here that there are ongoing movements that we must align ourselves with in the name of teaching and learning for joy and freedom. In fact, in moving one's teaching practice to be ever more in touch, we recognize that doing so can naturally help finesse your own role as an advocate to push against the very reasons classrooms may be out of touch to begin with.

How Did We Get Here and How Do We Get Out?

No teacher aspires to foster an out-of-touch teaching practice. The subtle shift, perhaps from one year to another, is incremental. Unreflective and unsupported teaching can naturally move in this direction; when we are not actively considering the needs of our students within the world around them, our teaching (and their learning) suffers.

In our own experience and in our work with teachers across the United States, we've seen out-of-touch teaching proliferate for several significant reasons that we feel it is important to name. Just as we acknowledge *why* being tuned in to students is imperative to improving equitable learning opportunities in all schools, we acknowledge that the lumbering of teachers into out-of-touch pedagogical practices is one that's often and invisibly imposed on our profession.

Increasingly the need for teachers to prepare students within classrooms is being narrowly defined through an emphasis on test taking that is high-stakes and stress-inducing. In many contexts, teacher evaluations are tied to student performance on such exams and, understandably, energy and attention can get devoted to preparing for and "teaching to" tests. This layer of accountability, from our perspective, gets in the way of powerful, present teaching practices. It also takes away teacher expertise. When the mandates on classrooms drive how we teach, the *why* of our profession is also uprooted.

> When the mandates on classrooms drive how we teach, the why of our profession is also uprooted.

Similar to the role of high-stakes testing and accountability, the serene picture of a quiet and "controlled" classroom might also pose a threat to innovative teaching practices. As educators, we are often guided to keep classes quiet—even when students, their hormones, and engaging curriculum might make students laugh and debate and move out of their seats enthusiastically and purposefully. Think back to some of the advice you may have heard in your first few years of teaching or even as a student teacher. Well-intentioned suggestions not to rock the boat within a new job are suggestions of how to fit into an often-archaic school culture rather than to forge into the uncharted waters of teaching in the present moment.

Furthermore, our classrooms often become out of touch because of a problem of stasis. Like many other aspects of schooling today, our classrooms often suffer beneath the weight of the expectations and demands placed upon them. It is an illusion that the lesson, text, assessment, or method that worked in the past remains the most ideal pedagogical approach for engaging young people in the present. We, as educators, remain lulled into a false belief that what worked in the past is always the right decision for the present. Whether it's having an out-of-body experience while teaching the symbolism in *Of Mice and Men* for the thirty-fifth time to students who are barely staying awake or questioning the lack of diversity described in the U.S. history curriculum, we know your classroom doesn't have to be mired in what was done in years prior.

The frustrations of this feeling of stuckness become compounded by the pressure to prepare students for outdated expectations of what college preparation means two decades into the twenty-first century. How students learn, participate, and *succeed* in college looks very different from approaches in the past, and this lack of clarity further unanchors today's secondary classrooms from the world that awaits young people beyond them.

As an example, in work encouraging students to write letters to the future president (in both 2016 and 2020), Garcia and his colleagues (2020) explored student letter writing and multimodal production. Building off partnership work led by the National Writing Project and KQED, an online platform allowed students to share their writing with a large public audience. This was standards-aligned writing that also allowed students to speak to topics they were interested in, advocate around particular issues of justice, and do so for an audience that was beyond the scope of singular classrooms. Much of this work dealt with complex disciplinary content knowledge in STEM subjects, such as climate change and—in 2020—the ways pandemics function globally. Though the project may, on its surface, look like something students have done year in and year out, this project utilized social media and prepared students for forms of civic engagement that are fundamentally different than in the past.

Finally, as a separate, equally important reason why out-of-touch teaching happens, we recognize that the world is constantly in motion. The trends, ideas, and modes of cultural production when teachers first entered the profession evolve, shift, and—in some cases—are forgotten. What might have been cutting-edge forms of "pedagogical content knowledge" (Shulman 1987) in one point in time might be deemed hackneyed or working at odds with the current fashions of teaching and learning.

The Pressure of Staying Up to Date

Keeping our classrooms tuned in to the demands of students that must receive the best possible education—not only for themselves but for strengthening the civic fabric that we send them out to weave—is a big demand. It is also a thrilling privilege for us as teachers: what an amazing opportunity it is to be able to positively transform and grow alongside students and the world today!

However, although this work can feel exhilarating and exhausting—perpetually trying to be mindful of the present to be tuned in to the lives of students—we think there is a more sustainable way to keep your instructional practices connected and relevant to the needs of young people today. In the section that follows, we'll detail some of the research on *why* teaching becomes out of touch as well as some of the key theories for how to transform our classrooms. We'll then use the last section of this book to focus on six key approaches that teachers can take today. We do not offer specific answers. Rather, this book was written in a time that has since become the past and we write with strategies for keeping your classroom living and breathing within the current needs of the students

See Section 2 for research on why teaching becomes out of touch and theories for how to transform classrooms.

before you. This is an invitation to learn and grow *alongside* the suggestions and research presented here. We hope you slide pedagogically into the wild possibilities of the present and transform your classroom for the societies of the future.

SECTION **2**

WHY ● NOT?

What Works?
Research for
Tuned-In Teaching

*A*s we discussed in the first section, *out-of-touch teaching* refers to pedagogical choices, interactions with students, and instructional materials that do not make an immediate and positive impact on the lives of students, that do not actively work to transform the social conditions of schooling, or that are disconnected from the interests and expertise of contemporary students in the present world. In this section, we discuss the research and rationales for infusing pedagogy with the following frameworks, practices, and value propositions: (1) critical pedagogy and culturally responsive and sustaining pedagogy, (2) digital literacies and youth popular culture, (3) Youth Participatory Action Research and youth voice, and (4) revolutionary love and mutually humanizing relationships.

Critical Pedagogy and Culturally Responsive Instruction

Critical pedagogy and culturally responsive/sustaining instruction are interrelated theories that we can draw on to transform our classrooms and move toward tuned-in teaching. Both theoretical frameworks focus on the students as having valuable knowledge and experiences that educators build upon to make meaningful bridges to the academic knowledge that we want students to learn and understand. Rather than viewing students' minds as empty receptacles waiting to be filled by their teachers, what Brazilian educator Paulo Freire (1970) called a "banking concept" of education, we should adopt a problem-posing education in which students, who are reconceptualized as intelligent and curious, and teachers work together to pose generative questions, to create meaningful dialogue, to develop collaborative projects, and ultimately to become agentive participants in social action designed to change the world. By learning to "read the word and read the world," students can give a name or label to the objects and ideas around them to talk about them and enact positive and liberating change. Freire (1970) offers a five-stage cyclical process to enact praxis (action and reflection): (1) identify a problem, (2) analyze a problem, (3) create a plan of action to address the problem, (4) implement the plan of action; and (5) analyze and evaluate the action. Through this process, students can become social agents who are "developing their capacity to confront real-world problems that face them and their community" and education becomes "a tool for eliminating oppressive relationships and conditions" (Duncan-Andrade and Morrell 2008, 14).

Many scholars have documented ways they and their students have enacted critical pedagogy in the classroom (e.g., Duncan-Andrade 2010; Emdin 2016; Cammarota and Fine 2008; Fisher 2007; Gutierrez 2008; Kirshner 2015; Lee 1995; McLaren 1989; Mirra, Garcia, and Morrell 2016; Rubin 2007). Jeff Duncan-Andrade and Ernest Morrell (2008) have written extensively on what critical pedagogy looks like with students both inside the traditional classroom and outside of school through summer programs, college access programs, and sports programs. One of many important points they share with audiences is that education often only focuses on the mastery of discrete facts and skills; however, "we know only too well that students can master these skills and succeed academically at great personal and social costs that include alienation from family, language, community, and progressive social values" (18). Instead, critical pedagogy, especially in urban schools, "strives to create spaces for students to learn as they also embrace and develop affirmed and empowered identities as intellectuals, as urban youth, and as members of historically marginalized ethnic groups" (18). Critical pedagogy does not dismiss the importance of mastering the skills that are treasured and measured in school; rather, critical pedagogues aim to help students become scholars in humanizing and empowering learning environments characterized by revolutionary love and centered on authentic, mutually respectful relationships (discussed further on pages 32–37).

> *Critical pedagogy does not dismiss the importance of mastering the skills that are treasured and measured in school; rather, critical pedagogues aim to help students become scholars in humanizing and empowering learning environments characterized by revolutionary love and centered on authentic, mutually respectful relationships.*

If a significant goal of critical pedagogy is to challenge social reproduction through schooling, then we must redress the differential access to cultural capital among individuals and groups, which permits some people more advantage (or exchange value) than others, perpetuating inequality under the disguise of a meritocratic and democratic state apparatus. Pierre Bourdieu (1986), a French social theorist, identifies three forms (or guises) of cultural capital, which include (1) embodied: manifested in the form of long-lasting dispositions of the mind and body, as in appearance, speech, ways of being; (2) objectified: acquired via exclusive access to elite cultural goods such as photographs, books, dictionaries, and libraries, or music instruments, and so on; and (3) institutionalized: obtained in the form of certifications such as educational degrees, licenses, and credentials. These three forms of capital can be exchanged for advantage and access, actualized in economic and material well-being. Under the logic of social reproduction, each generation reproduces the same socioeconomic status of the previous generation due to

the type and amount of capital they receive and are able
to pass on to the next generation (Bourdieu 1986; Willis
1977). Italian sociologist Antonio Gramsci (1971) identified
school as the institution playing the most significant role
in perpetuating social reproduction. When students attend
high-resourced schools, they often have access to more
resources, or "capital," from the number of books in their
classroom libraries, age and quality of teaching materials,
low teacher and leadership turnover, additional funds
from families and the community through fundraisers,
extracurricular activities, quality and access to technology,
and so on. For students coming from homes with the
forms of capital valued most in society, schools maintain
and extend the exchange value of their cultural capital.
The inverse is often the case in low-resourced schools that
experience higher teacher and leadership turnover (Anyon
1981; Noguera 2003; Valenzuela 1999), older buildings
and materials, less access to technology, and a denigration
of their language, family, and community (Campano 2007;
Moll et al. 1992) or their community cultural wealth (Yosso
2006). This is not accidental or coincidental. Schools,
particularly urban schools, perpetuate social reproduction
and inequality (Duke 2000; Noguera 2003). Bourdieu (1986)
concurs and has argued that cultural capital explains the

> See Section 3 for classroom
> examples of critical pedagogy.

unequal academic achievement of children
originating from historically vulnerable
social classes (3). However, with critical
pedagogy, students and teachers work
collaboratively to identify, name, and challenge dominant
narratives, ideologies, and inequities woven into the
education system, hopefully increasing the exchange value
of their capital for academic success, personal actualization,
and civic engagement. Curious about what this actually
looks like in classrooms? We explore several strategies for
taking up these ideas in the next section of this book.

Similar to critical pedagogy, culturally responsive or culturally sustaining pedagogy is focused on the students and honors the knowledge, perspectives, and experiences they bring to the classroom. Scholars such as Gloria Ladson-Billings, James Banks, Geneva Gay, Christine Sleeter, Carl Grant, Sonia Nieto, Patty Bode, Django Paris, and Sammy Alim have written extensively on how students are members of multiple cultures outside of school, and when educators recognize these various cultures, while also appreciating the individuality of each student, the classroom becomes a more humanizing space. In her landmark study of eight teachers whom she called the "Dreamkeepers," because they were extremely successful in teaching African American children, Ladson-Billings (2009) shows how each teacher identified and built upon the strengths of their students. The teachers ensured the students experienced academic success by focusing on three central tenets, "student learning, developing cultural competence, and cultivating a sociopolitical awareness in their students" (xi). They respected the cultural competences of their students and wove aspects of their students' culture into the curriculum to help the students make sense of the world and to learn. In this way, they were being culturally responsive to their students' out-of-school lives and using their students' rich culture to make in-school knowledge more accessible. Worth noting is that the eight teachers in Ladson-Billings' study were of various ethnic backgrounds and geographical regions. They had attended a variety of colleges and universities. They were not necessarily members of their students' out-of-school cultural groups; rather, they embraced their children and saw each one as a learner and as a member of a vibrant, rich, and loving cultural community.

Just as culturally relevant pedagogy, culturally responsive pedagogy, and culturally sustaining pedagogy (terms are often used interchangeably) are most closely connected with

Gloria Ladson-Billings' work, multicultural education is first associated with the scholarship of James Banks. Drawing on the work of earlier scholars like W. E. B. DuBois and Carter G. Woodson (author of *Miseducation of the Negro* in 1922), James Banks (1996) championed multicultural education which focuses on creating equitable and sustaining educational opportunities for children of all racial, ethnic, and social classes, by honoring and incorporating historical perspectives, diverse texts, ideas, ways of learning, and ways of being from a multitude of cultures into the curriculum and pedagogical approaches of the classroom. Moving beyond the potluck or once-a-year holiday celebration, multicultural education is committed to empowering historically marginalized groups. It allows, even fosters, access to a higher and fuller humanity of the members of historically dominant groups by incorporating diverse cultures and perspectives into a polyvocal curriculum, teachers' pedagogy, and school culture. Banks' five dimensions of multicultural education include (1) content integration; (2) the knowledge construction process; (3) prejudice reduction; (4) an equity pedagogy; and (5) an empowering school culture and social structure. Although each dimension is conceptually distinct, in practice they overlap and are interrelated (Banks 1996).

A newer strand of research, that combines culturally responsive instruction, applied linguistics, bilingual education, funds of knowledge, critical pedagogy, and multilingualism, is translanguaging. Pioneered by Ofelia García (García 2009; García and Li Wei 2014) and others, translanguaging pedagogy and research seek to destabilize dominant understandings of monolingualism that underpin K–12 school culture. Translanguaging works to foreground bi/multilingualism as both the historical norm and as ubiquitous (Canagarajah 1999; García 2009; Seltzer and de los Ríos 2021). Translanguaging, different from code-switching or code-meshing, describes environments where students can leverage simultaneous linguistic repertoires into an integrated and fluid communication system where multiple methods of expressing, or languaging, can sit alongside one another in an equitable and humanizing polyvocality. These scholars argue that multilingualism is a strength of students and should be incorporated into dynamic classroom instruction that is truly responsive to the cultural and linguistic heterogeneity of contemporary students and classrooms. In *The Translanguaging Classroom: Leveraging Student Bilingualism for Learning*, Garcia, Johnson, and Seltzer (2017) offer innovative strategies for teachers to use translanguaging in their classrooms to increase identity development and student achievement. In their 2017 article "Translanguaging, Coloniality, and English Classrooms: An Exploration of Two Bicoastal Urban Classrooms" de los Ríos and Seltzer highlight contexts for learning that help linguistically marginalized students thrive academically, culturally, and socially in two urban English classrooms. They explore the concept of translanguaging through the writing of two students who took up this practice as a challenge to coloniality in English classrooms. They also outline how secondary teachers in New York City and Los Angeles adopted a translanguaging pedagogy to the academic and social benefit of their students.

By seeing the individuality and unique cultures of each student, as well as the similarities that unite us such as shared cultural practices, we can identify and build upon our students' strengths, knowledge, and experiences to make learning more engaging and relevant.

Rather than thinking about critical or culturally responsive pedagogy as most beneficial for students who continue to score lower than peers on standardized tests and other school-sanctioned measures, we can think of these approaches as valuable for all students, and as ways to transform out-of-touch teaching. By seeing the individuality and unique cultures of each student, as well as the similarities that unite us, such as shared cultural practices, we can identify and build upon our students' strengths, knowledge, and experiences to make learning more engaging and relevant.

We should begin with the premise that all students can learn—after all, even our youngest learners possess language and literacies that are extremely complex and difficult to acquire. Critical linguists Donaldo Macedo (2019), Geneva Smitherman (1999), and H. Samy Alim (2006) urge educators to acknowledge the beauty and depth of students' linguistic competence, particularly those languages that are made invisible or even tarnished in the public discourse. Alim, Smitherman, and Macedo remind us of the complexity and human genius inherent in the myriad language practices of our students. In "Beyond the Methods Fetish: Toward a Humanizing Pedagogy," Lilia Bartolomé (1994) argues for a humanizing pedagogy that respects and uses the language, reality, history, and perspectives of students as an integral part of educational practice. Bartolomé emphasizes the need for teachers' evolving political awareness of their relationship with students as knowers and active participants in their own learning.

Therefore, the onus falls on us to create learning environments that honor students' choices, voices, and multiple cultural communities. Our students' multicultural and multilingual identities should be woven into the curriculum and daily classroom activities and discussions. As educators, we need to remember that cultures are not static; rather, they are fluid and changing, and culturally responsive instruction is a curriculum *and* a pedagogy. No curricular artifact, by itself, is culturally responsive. Therefore, it is the responsibility of the educator to make the curriculum relevant and representative of the students.

In my (Ernest's) more recent work, I draw upon critical pedagogy and culturally responsive instruction to offer twelve suggestions of research driven practices in prekindergarten to grade 12 literacy instruction (in all subject areas):

1. Student choice in independent reading

2. Interactive teacher-led discussions

3. Multicultural literature and multicultural readings of literature

4. Polyvocal classrooms that honor student voice and multilingualism

5. Incorporating youth popular culture

6. Interest-driven research projects

7. Writing across genres (traditional and multimodal)

8. Critical media literacies

9. Youth Participatory Action Research

10. Writing for authentic audiences in multiple voices and multiple languages

11. Inquiry-based instruction

12. Diverse classroom libraries

Digital Literacies and Youth Popular Culture

In a study by Common Sense Media, researchers Rideout and Robb (2019) found that of the 1,600 participants, tweens (ages 8–12 years old) spent approximately four hours and forty-four minutes and teens (ages 13–18 years old) spent approximately seven hours and twenty-two minutes each day engaged on "entertainment screen media" (not including for school or homework). When accounting for socioeconomic status, researchers found a significant difference in use. Tweens and teens from higher-income homes "use an hour and 50 minutes less screen media per day than those from lower-income households" (5). Per day! If we consider the subtle and implicit messages in media that perpetuate dominant narratives that reinforce negative stereotypes based on race/ethnicity, socioeconomics, and gender, these statistics are even more disturbing since race/ethnicity and class are so closely correlated. Finally, researchers found that "online video viewing is through the roof: More than twice as many young people watch videos every day than did in 2015, and the average time spent watching has roughly doubled" (3).

Although there are benefits and advantages to having access to and engaging in entertainment screen media and developing digital literacies, the American Medical Association (AMA) and the American Academy of Pediatrics (AAP) (Reid 2016) have cautioned adults and children about the possible negative side effects and health outcomes of overexposure to uncritical consumption of mainstream media. Some of these outcomes include obesity, sleep problems, depression, anxiety, and eating disorders. Rather than eliminating media, both the AMA and AAP have called on educators to address media use with their students and to help young people to become more conscious consumers.

The AMA and AAP concerns are as old as the wise counsel provided by the Frankfurt School social theorists Walter Benjamin (1935) and Theodor Adorno and Max Horkheimer (1944) in the 1930s and 1940s, who saw the potential of the media to cause anxiety and paranoia as means to shape the behavior of the masses. Later, scholars such as Douglass Kellner (1995) and Baudrillard (2001) continued this work, showing how the corporate media work to instill a commodity culture that is largely predicated upon an addicted and unsuspecting class of youth. However, a second tradition of scholars has looked

We want students, as critical consumers, to understand how they are being influenced by often subtle, but sometimes overt, messages from the media. Ultimately, though, we want students who also understand their agency via media production, dissemination, and invention.

to hip-hop culture (Alim 2006), film (Morrell 2004), radio (Soepp and Chavez 2010), spoken word poetry (Fisher 2007), video gaming (Gee 2003), and social media (Ito et al. 2009) as sites of youth participatory culture (Jenkins et al. 2009) engagement, agency, and resistance. Although still wary of the potentially ill effects of media use, this latter group is much more optimistic about critical media literacy as an act of a critical and culturally responsive approach to literacy instruction. We don't take a side in this debate; we want students to critically engage the media in their lives to better understand the potential and the peril of how power is used to either perpetuate or challenge inequities. We want students, as critical consumers, to understand how they are being influenced by often subtle, but sometimes overt, messages from the media. Ultimately, though, we want students who also understand their agency via media production, dissemination, and invention. Just to be clear, digital and critical literacies are not simply a needed emphasis in English language arts classrooms alone. This is work that is vital across every classroom students enter today.

Nicole Mirra, Ernest Morrell, and Danielle Filipiak (2018) offer four dimensions of critical media pedagogy that help students not just to consume media, but also to create and disseminate their own media productions. The teaching of media and digital literacies has gained increased attention in the twenty years following the New London Group's land-mark *Harvard Educational Review* publication "A Pedagogy of Multiliteracies: Designing Social Futures" (1996). From approaches urging the study of popular culture to calls for youth-led social media revolution, there is no shortage of approaches. Yet scant attention is offered toward articulating a new and comprehensive theory of pedagogy and produc-tion that acknowledges the changing tools and technologies at young people's disposal, conceptualizes young people as media producers, and applies these developments to today's complex classroom context. Mirra, Morrell, and Filipiak (2018) articulate a new critical theory of multiliteracies that encompasses four types of digital engagement: (1) critical digital consumption, (2) critical digital production, (3) critical distribution, and (4) critical digital invention. We make the argument that a new critical theory of multi-literacies needs to account for each of these types of digital engagement. Ultimately, however, we must move beyond theorizing our youth as passive consumers or even critical users of digital technologies, and move toward the project of facilitating youth communities of digital innovation.

When we think about digital literacies, we typically think about the first dimension—consumption. In their 2019 report on media use by teens and tweens, Rideout and Robb found that "despite the new affordances and promises of digital devices, young people devote very little time to creating their own content" (6). Teens devote about 39 percent of their time viewing TV or videos, 22 percent to gaming, 16 percent to social media, 4 percent video chatting, 2 percent e-reading, and only 3 percent creating their own writing, art, or music. Rideout and Robb report this is virtually unchanged since the 2015 findings. Given these disconcerting statistics, Mirra, Morrell, and Filipiak's (2018) call to help students become critical consumers is extremely important and even more timely these days. How do we help students ask questions about the media in our lives, and how do we have conversations with others about the media we consume? Teachers and students analyze not only the text itself—whether this is a TV show, video, video game—but also the roles of the creator, the audience, and the stakeholders with interest in this power relationship. They can also have explicit conversations about visual literacies and digital rhetorics.

The second dimension is production. Rather than pursue a limited media literacy approach, which encourages students to write about media and perhaps utilize the tools of media to do so, Mirra, Morrell, and Filipiak (2018) argue for production under the banner of critical media literacy. They cite Kellner and Share's (2007) discussion of critical media literacy, which states, "Critical media literacy thus constitutes a critique of mainstream approaches to literacy and a political project for democratic social change. This involves a multi-perspectival critical inquiry, of popular culture and the culture industries, that addresses issues of class, race, gender, sexuality, and power and also promotes the production of alternative counter-hegemonic media" (8–9). Production is more than a written review of media. Production within a critical media literacy approach questions normative ideologies, or what we have taken for granted to be the "norm" without questioning who benefits, who is harmed, and how these ideologies have been created and perpetuated. In Section 3, we look at several approaches to include youth voice and center complex media production across subject areas; such approaches are not only possible in your classroom but vibrantly engaging.

The third dimension is distribution. It is now possible to distribute products at unprecedented scale across time and space to vast audiences, which means authentic engagement with individuals outside of the traditional classroom space. This creates unique chances for students to learn how to analyze their audiences and for teachers to help students create opportunities for students to share through various platforms and social media sites. Research suggests that writing for such authentic audiences leads to better writing (Block and Strachan 2019). Through this type of invention and distribution, we re-envision young people as inventors with competencies and dispositions to dream up digital forms of expression that adults cannot yet imagine. It also allows us to focus on equity and consider what we should do differently to provide all children with the opportunity to design and build digital technologies of the future.

The final dimension is invention and, well, we're not there yet—at least not consistently across all content areas. We can see powerful examples of critical digital engagement in some recent computer science instruction that considers computational literacy practices that can uplift community learning (Lee and Soep 2016). In the ways that these digital practices forge together the humanities and social sciences, we recognize that digital invention requires constantly considering the current moment and its pedagogical demands.

Through these four dimensions of developing digital literacies (consumption, production, distribution, and invention) and texts viewed through a critical media literacy lens, we help students to hone their analytic skills and ask questions about whose values or ideas are being promoted (what does it mean to be normal, what does it mean to have power, what does it mean to be desired, who is marginalized or "othered") and how audiences or recipients are constructed (who is targeted, what assumptions are made about the audience, how the ad/image/artifact intends to make the recipient feel about him- or herself, what an audience member is compelled to do/believe).

As we help students to become critical consumers and developers of texts, we can make meaningful and explicit connections to youth popular culture. These days, perhaps the most obvious and ubiquitous forms of youth popular culture is connected to social media. Given the amount of time teens and tweens spend on entertainment screen media (tweens: four hours and forty-four minutes; teens: seven hours and twenty-two minutes), it is not surprising that popular culture is shared widely through digital devices. Although the amount of time devoted to social media over the past five years has not changed significantly, the age at which teens and tweens first use social media is younger. Among sixteen- to eighteen-year-olds who use social media, "the median age of first use is 14; twenty-eight percent say they started before 13, 43% at 13 or 14 years old, and 30% not until they were 15 or older" (Rideout and Robb 2019, 6). Although many reports and data can be alarming, again, we take a balanced view of the benefits and possible problems with social media. If young people are not taught to read social media through a critical lens, the subtle and/ or overt messages can have long-term damaging effects, such as lower self-esteem. However, when youth are viewing texts with a critical eye, they become members of youth culture in positive and uplifting ways. They can become part of communities that share their interests, values, and beliefs. They can co-construct new ideas and challenge archaic notions and negative stereotypes about teens. Although some may lament and wish for the past or use crisis language, if we look at how young people

> For more on how to get in touch with your students' digital lives, see Section 3, pages 53–55.

are using digital literacy and creating youth culture, it's quite impressive. Young people are savvy with social media. They are making connections with other youth near and far. Instead of fretting because teens say they "read for pleasure less than once a month, if at all" or hoping we have enough informational text in our curriculum to meet standards, let's recognize that the majority of internet material is informational in nature.

Youth Participatory Action Research and Youth Voice

We have a tremendous body of research on the experiences of youth within and outside of school; yet the actual voices of the youth being studied are typically silenced or simply absent. Youth Participatory Action Research (YPAR) is unique in that those most impacted by this educational research, the youth, become the researchers. As empowered participants, their inquiries and voices are at the heart of the research.

YPAR is also unique in that the inquiry centers on youth's expertise. Through action research, they become producers of knowledge and agents of change (Bautista et al. 2013).

YPAR is considered a subcategory of Participatory Action Research (PAR) and represents "a radical shift from traditional research because of *what* it investigates and *who* does the investigating" (Morrell 2006, 112–13). YPAR is "critical," "participatory," and "action-oriented" in that it "challenges the hierarchy of knowledge production and changes the relationship of knowledge producers to knowledge consumers" (Morrell 2006, 3). Although PAR is not a new research approach, a critical perspective and approach with youth as the subjects rather than the objects certainly is.

We can trace PAR to Kurt Lewin, a German-American social psychologist who conceptualized and enacted action research in the late 1930s with quasi-experimental tests in factory and neighborhood settings (Adelman 1993, 7). He and his graduate students were particularly interested in raising the self-esteem of minority groups via action research with a strong emphasis on participation. His research was described as practical experiences and focused on power, reflective thought, discussion, decision, and action by "ordinary" people. Lewin believed that action research could inform social planning and action, and so he developed a theory of action research as "proceeding in a spiral of steps, each of which is composed of planning, action and the evaluation of the result of action" (Kemmis and McTaggert 1990, 8). PAR also draws on the philosophy of educational theorist John Dewey, that schools can act as the agency of democratic change within communities. Dewey was focused on teachers and believed that experimental inquiry should inform social practice and in turn become directed practical doing (Dewey 1902). By reflecting on their practice, Dewey suggested that teachers could be actively involved in curriculum development and educational reform (Dewey 1902). If we apply Dewey's theory to YPAR, in which young people are engaged in experimental inquiry, the intentions of the outcomes remain the same. Findings from YPAR can also play an active role in curriculum development and educational reform when educators, curriculum developers, and policy makers take young people's research seriously and draw on the new knowledge and findings to transform pedagogy and the educational system.

More recently, McIntyre (2000) offered three principles that guide most PAR projects: (1) the collective investigation of a problem; (2) the reliance on indigenous knowledge to better understand that problem; and (3) the desire to take individual and/or collective action to deal with the stated problem. Similar to Lewin's belief, McIntyre suggests that when participants become researchers about their daily lives, in hopes of developing realistic solutions for dealing with the problems that they believe need to be addressed, their active and full involvement in the research process gives them the opportunity to mobilize, organize, and implement individual and/or collective action (Selener [1997] as cited in Morrell [2006]).

Although the conceptualization and initial enactments of PAR are often credited to two leading American scholars and philosophers, Lewin and Dewey, Morrow and Torres (1995) discuss how it gained recognition in Latin America through the Symposium of Cartagena on Critical Social Science Research in April 1977 and "the influence of Brazilian educator Paulo Freire (1970) who engaged marginalized populations of Brazilian peasants as collaborators, researchers, and activists" (Morrell 2006, 6). Freire's revolutionary pedagogy helped historically overlooked people develop critical literacy and inquiry skills to address structures of power. The idea of employing inquiry for advocacy is, as Ernest (Morrell 2006) says, "as old as the tradition of inquiry itself" and reminds us that "this is important to keep in mind amid contemporary conversations about quality, validity, and rigor in social scientific research" (6).

We have many examples of international PAR projects as collaborations between sanctioned institutions and local groups, but our work, critical YPAR, focuses on young people and their voice. So how is student voice connected to YPAR? Youth voice is at the core of PAR. The researchers, in this case young people, identify a specific topic or issue, design their study, collect and analyze data, and arrive at research findings. Ideally they will have an audience with whom to share their findings to make substantive, positive changes (Morrell 2004). Throughout this process the youth are supported by adults who can guide them as they identify their specific topics and throughout the research and dissemination process. Yet the most important aspect of this research is the students' or young people's voices. They identify the topic of research—what matters most to them, what impacts their lives in substantial ways, what needs to change, how they want to be change agents, and so on. They voice their opinions and insights on what type of data should be gathered, by whom, and how. They bring their unique perspectives to the data as empowered participants. Audiences hear the voices of young people sharing findings and suggesting action for change. This is what makes YPAR so powerful—those most impacted by the research are the researchers themselves. We will see examples of enacting this work in Section 3 of this book.

Youth voice is at the core of participatory action research.

For examples of what it looks like to enact YPAR in classrooms, see Section 3, pp 61–65.

We are happy to report that YPAR is increasingly being taken seriously in the research community, with results that speak powerfully to its potential to engage young people and to impact life in neighborhoods and communities. In 2008 Julio Camarrota and Michelle Fine co-edited *Revolutionizing Education: Youth Participatory Action Research in Motion*, which brought together (in Morrell 2006 when Ernest and his research team began using the term *Youth Participatory Action Research*) several projects in Arizona, New York, and California to discuss our work, its influences, and most importantly, our common ground. From that meeting the idea of collectively referring to the work as *Youth Participatory Action Research* stuck. Several of those contributors (Shawn Ginwright, Beth Rubin, Eve Tuck, Ben Kirshner, Maria Elena Torre, Ernest Morrell, Augustin Romero) have produced volumes in the ensuing years that have shaped our understanding of YPAR and its contributions to an educational field that is increasingly interested in engagement, youth production, and social action. Caraballo and colleagues (2017) coauthored "YPAR and Critical Epistemologies: Rethinking Education Research" for the American Educational Research Association publication *Review of Research in Education,* which outlines the foundations of YPAR and examines the distinct epistemological, methodological, and pedagogical contributions of an interdisciplinary corpus of YPAR studies and scholarship. The authors outline the origins and disciplines of YPAR and make a case for its role in education research, discuss its contributions to the field and the tensions and possibilities of YPAR across disciplines. They close by proposing a YPAR critical-epistemological framework that centers youth and their communities, alongside practitioners, scholars, and researchers, as knowledge producers and change agents for social justice.

Finally, why does voice matter? We spend 70 to 80 percent of our waking hours in some form of communication (Hyslop and Tone 1989) and 75 percent of that time is spent speaking and listening. Classrooms are a unique space, typically a room with one adult and upward of thirty students for up to six hours each day. It's difficult to think of another confined space with so many bodies for so much time. We might wonder if it's possible to hear every voice, especially in a traditional sense of "speaking." Although we value time and space for all students to speak their ideas and inquiries, which can happen in small groups, we think about student voice, or youth voice, as emanating through a myriad of forms to a wide audience. When students are engaged in YPAR, their voices and ideas are guiding the research from inception to presentation and dissemination.

Centering Love and Relationships

Angela Valenzuela (1999) begins her book *Subtractive Schooling* with a quote from a ninth grader that reads, "If the *school* doesn't care about my learning, why should *I* care? Answer me that. Just answer me that!" (3). As an educator, our immediate response may be shock or to quickly defend ourselves and our colleagues and distance ourselves from a school, teachers, and a system that would generate this type of response from a child. But before we respond in this way, let us assume validity and possible reasons behind this student's critique. How we feel as the educator, or what we believe we are conveying to our students, may not be as important as how our students feel and interpret interactions. Valenzuela challenges her reader by stating, "What if each weekday, for eight hours a day, teenagers inhabited a world populated by adults who did not care—or at least did not care for *them* sufficiently?" Rather than dismissing this student's raw and candid response, let's start by thinking about how to ensure that no child utters these words.

Teaching is about relationships. Educational psychologist Asa Hilliard stated, "I have never encountered any children in any group who are not geniuses. There is no mystery on how to teach them. The first thing you do is treat them like human beings and the second thing you do is love them" (In Morrell, 2015, 3). He does not mention the best lesson plan or increasing standardized test scores, based largely on material that students are not likely to remember after they leave school. But they will remember how we made them feel about themselves, their families, and their communities outside of school. We should also contemplate findings from Valenzuela's (1999) work, in particular the education system's role in perpetuating poor academic performance. Rather than "dismissing urban, U.S.-born youth as lazy underachievers," she encourages researchers and practitioners to consider that these young people are "neither inherently anti school nor oppositional. They oppose a schooling process that disrespects them; they oppose not education, but *schooling*" (5). More specifically, when discussing the experiences of Black children, Johnson, Bryan and Boutte (2019) state that "when Black children are 'educated' rather than 'schooled' they become revolutionaries who push back against the intentional and unintentional anti-Black violence and social reproduction (Shujaa 1994) constructed to keep them at what Bell (1992) referred to as 'the bottom of the well' or society's lowest rungs" (55). We would be hard-pressed to find a parent who does not care about their child's education or want the best education for their child. As Valenzuela and many other scholars have shared with their scholarship, inequitable, often harmful, schooling is what parents and children oppose, not an education.

Although Valenzuela was focused on the experiences of Latinx youth, we can find similar sentiments in communities that are often viewed through a deficit lens. In the conclusion of their edited book *Educating Harlem*, Erickson and Morrell (2020) discuss the long and consistent struggle of educators and community members in Harlem, a historically and predominantly Black community, to provide a meaningful and helpful education to the children of Harlem. Since the 1920s, parents and community members have been pushing back on restrictive curriculum, structural constraints, material inequities, and persistent racism—hardly an opposition to education. For these two historically marginalized groups, Black Americans and Mexican Americans or Latinx populations, education has been deeply valued and often a long and exhausting battle for families to get the type of education their children deserve. We see from these communities that their desire for education is not lacking, but rather their desire to be valued and cared for within a school system that perpetuates inequalities is overlooked. The most significant missing piece is the students' feeling of being cared for by the adults in their educational lives. While analyzing data from her study of Latinx youth at a high school in Houston, Texas, Valenzuela was struck by how often the words *care*, *caring*, and *caring for* appeared in her field notes (7). Simply stated, students want to feel cared for in school.

What does this look like in the classroom? It is easy and understandable to be overwhelmed by a focus on standards and high-stakes testing, a narrow curriculum, limited resources, an overcrowded classroom—we could go on with the list of challenges. Practitioners may not control the purse strings or the curriculum or testing schedule, but we do control the classroom culture and how kids are made to feel about themselves. Scholars such as Duncan-Andrade (2010), who draws on Valenzuela's (1999) work, argue for *cariño* (an authentic caring) across all facets of the education field, from the everyday classroom to educational research. He argues for making the voices of students heard to inform our practices as teachers, coaches, and researchers (see also Howard, Milner-McCall, and Howard [2020]).

How do we do this? Allyn and Morrell (2016) focus on seven social-emotional strengths (belonging, curiosity, friendship, kindness, confidence, courage, and hope) as

> *Practitioners may not control the purse strings or the curriculum or testing schedule, but we do control the classroom culture and how kids are made to feel about themselves.*

critical components of any classroom culture if we want our students to thrive emotionally, socially, and academically. Drawing on a long and extensive body of research on the importance of a child's social-emotional development as a means to overall success and well-being, they argue for building a safe and loving environment to help children become "forever-learners," which will help them to be college- and career-ready, terms we hear often in relation to standards—but more importantly, to become actively involved members of civic life. By beginning with an assets-based model, focusing on what children *can* do, Allyn and Morrell are adamant about shifting our current paradigm from discourse and a focus on perceived deficits to capitalizing and building children's strength. We do this by focusing on positive nurturing relationships between students and between the teacher(s) and students that put social and emotional needs ahead of test scores and rigid standards. We are not encouraging educators to ignore the academic skills that are measured and treasured by traditional schooling, but instead to put more time and energy into developing humanizing learning spaces where every child is valued and authentic caring guides interactions, planning, and instruction. When students feel valued, they learn more.

Pedagogy that centers love and relationships or connects love and revolution may make educators uncomfortable. To clarify, when we discuss love, we are not referring to the secondary definitions found in Merriam-Webster's Dictionary, which emphasize attraction based on sexual desire: the strong affection and tenderness felt by lovers or a beloved person. Rather, we are focused on the primary definition, which is "a quality or feeling of strong or constant affection for and dedication to another" (Merriam-Webster 2020), and also Chabot's (2008) deeper understanding of love. He states, "I argue that we need to focus more directly on *human relationships* between (or within) individuals and groups" (808). Citing Gould (1978), Chabot adds that genuine love "involves connections among social individuals who work together toward a common purpose while validating each person's uniqueness" (809).

Connecting *love* and *revolution* may seem odd or even impossible if we only associate revolutions with anger and protests. In discussing their theory of a transformational political concept of love in critical education, Lanas and Zembylas (2015) recognize that "when we build on anger, we get anger; when we build on love, love is what we get" (32). We can also consider Johnson, Bryan, and Boutte's (2019) question, "What would it look like to (re)imagine urban classrooms as sites of love?" (46) and to eliminate simple and superficial notions of love such as "I love all children regardless of if they are Black, white or purple" (48) to end "fake love" and fill classrooms with humanizing love. We can start with Hilliard's advice (Morrell 2015, 326), to see all children as geniuses and human beings and to love them.

The Practice of Revolutionary Love

What's love got to do with it? Everything! Everything! It is a term that we do not like to talk about. The curriculum, the lesson plans, the amazing, diverse literature that you put in someone's hands means nothing if you do not love that person. What does revolutionary love mean when it is manifested by an English teacher? That is the difference. That we believe in them. That them failing is us failing. We are operating in the public trust. How many hours do I leave my children with other people and expect them to feel loved in the same way as they would in their own home? I, like the parents of the other 50 million children who are in the school system. Love has everything to do with it! It does not work without love!

—Ernest Morrell's 2014 NCTE Presidential Address (2015)

To begin his Critical Pedagogy course in the spring of 2021, Ernest asked his students what one word they most associated with powerful teaching. The two words that emerged on the digital word cloud they created were *love* and *empowerment*. Ernest mentioned to his class that he saw these two words as sides of the same coin. Love, at least revolutionary love, is often defined by what you can help someone else to become or actualize. At Columbia University, where Ernest was a director from 2011 to 2017, his students designated 2017 as the year of revolutionary love.

We think of this in three ways. How do we use our talents to promote a love of self? So many problems in the fields of health, wellness, and education stem from a lack of self-love that a major task for educators is to make the students we encounter feel loved and valued, as if they have something important to contribute. Because they do. A second practice of revolutionary love is enacting kindness toward others in our immediate vicinity. How do we manifest this kindness and how do we promote it? What does it mean to exhibit kindness in the classroom and in our social circles? What does it look like to practice kindness via the discipline of English, history, math, or whatever subject area you teach? Stress is a social toxin and it dehumanizes. In moments of stress the brain becomes a nonessential organ and people are less able to think or act rationally. How will you contribute to or alleviate stress in others?

And finally, the third practice of revolutionary love is true engagement with the world. How do you work to provide for others what you want for yourself and those you care for? At the end of the day what we all want is essentially the same. And, like John Lennon, we, Antero and Ernest, are dreamers enough to believe that it is possible for all of us in the human family to have what we need in this life. But it won't happen unless we collectively practice revolutionary love.

Famous American novelist and public intellectual Toni Morrison has said that "if there is a book that you want to read and it hasn't been written yet, then you must write it" (In Morrell, 2015). If we think of all the wonderful lives, the books that have been written in words and deeds, the giants in our families and on our bookshelves whose shoulders we stand upon, there is only one option, and that is to act.

What books will you write with your pedagogical life?

SECTION **3**

BUT ● **THAT**

*Sustaining the
Tuned-In Classroom*

ANTERO GARCIA AND ERNEST MORRELL

*T*hroughout this book, we have highlighted the pitfalls of out-of-touch teaching and looked at the research that suggests the need for making yours a more responsive and engaging classroom. However, putting such steps into action can often feel challenging. We offer a road map for beginning to intentionally change yours into a classroom that is transformative for your students and revitalizing for you. As we describe six different primary and important steps toward transforming your class into an active, just, and in-touch space, we offer two important caveats.

First, no magic bullet can slay the inequities and long-standing legacies of racism that shape what Gloria Ladson-Billings (2009) refers to as an "educational debt." Similarly, there is no easy answer to making school relevant and engaging for every learner. Taken together, the actions in this part of the book will not single-handedly transform the realm of public education. Rather, they are necessary steps and reaffirm your commitments to the humanizing needs of learning in your district, school, or classroom today. Furthermore, we write the following actions to challenge the notion that there are broad and singular best practices that can be blindly applied to classrooms whole cloth. Instead, we know that your context for teaching shifts minute by minute, year by year, and looks vastly different from a teacher in another area of the country or even your district (Garcia and O'Donnell-Allen 2015). Though the following actions high-light deliberate strategies for classroom engagement, you will not find a simple formula. We believe in your expertise in harnessing these marching orders—as we refer to them when working with young people in Youth Participatory Action Research projects (Mirra, Garcia, and Morrell 2016)—for your specific context and community.

Second, these are not actions that exist isolated from one another. Centering the knowledge and interests of students (action #1) does not happen independently of maintaining classrooms as spaces of production (action #5). We describe classrooms that seek to build an intersection of related pedagogical practices. These collectively construct an ethos of just and tuned-in teaching. Though you may wrestle with some of the suggestions here—perhaps they look wildly different from your assumptions of what teaching looks like—we encourage you to experiment, deviate, and remix the actions here to fit your needs and comfort level as a continually growing and learning educator. Rather than a recipe book for concocting the perfect classroom, see these actions as guidance for you to customize and tailor your instruction to the passions and uncertainties that are in the hearts of your students.

Action #1: Students at the Center

Up to now we've pointed to critical and historical traditions about *why* your teaching practice needs to be tuned in. As we look at specific ways to make your teaching more engaging, perhaps the most important step is centering your students, their lives, interests, passions, and hopes. Just as we might find ourselves inadvertently tuning out at a dinner party when the conversation turns to something outside of our experience or interests, if students don't see themselves—constantly—in texts you teach, in the discussions you facilitate, and in the kinds of writing tasks you assign, classroom life is inherently out of touch with who your students are. What's worse, without taking some of the fundamental steps we describe here, assuming who your students are without doing the work of getting to know them can make schools alien and sources of stereotypes.

There is an implicit question you need to con
you design to make your classroom a more tune
For whom? A tuned-in learning environment ne
student-facing, even if this means the texts,
questions, and jargon feel strange to you
as an adult facilitator of a primarily youth-
embodied space. Ideally, you are building
work that addresses grand questions about
the world in its present state, and a collective
set of activities for improvement writ large of
this world. However, if that feels like too big
a task to tackle right now, starting with the
primary interests of your students is more
than enough. Though this section focuses
primarily on steps for establishing your
classroom as a student-centered space, we'll elaborate on how
this work is sustained across tuned-in approaches to critical
instruction later in this chapter as well.

> *A tuned-in learning environment needs to be student-facing, even if this means the texts, questions, and jargon feel strange to you as an adult facilitator of a primarily youth-embodied space.*

Seeing Your Class

Getting to know your students begins with a couple of
simple foundational beliefs that we think should help guide
nearly every action in your classroom:

1. Every single student in your class is different.

2. Earning your students' individual and collective trust
   means seeing and acknowledging them as brilliant,
   creative, full of emotions, and socially important.

Every student in your class needs to feel like they are the
most important student in your curriculum and they need to
feel that every. single. day.

The collective enterprise of education must be for preparing students to better lead in our unknown future. Having
students see themselves in this work is key, and this means
that the first days of your classroom should be times for

alking, learning, and building together a vision of what life in this classroom space will look like for the rest of the year. It is easy to pay lip service to your classroom feeling like a family and it is easy to say you care for your students, but neither of these things can be true if you can't actually see and understand who each of your students is.

Our colleague Patrick Camangian wrote about the powerful role that autoethnography played in shaping a critical context for learning in his classroom (2010). As a writing practice in which students describe their lived experiences in relation to the world around them, autoethnography can function as an important writing task for getting to know your students, building trust with them, and providing space for them to feel affirmed and valued in your classroom. Importantly, these writing practices are not divorced from the academic goals of classrooms. In Camangian's context, his students reflected on the world around them and produced complex, standards-aligned narratives that illuminated their growing understanding of sociopolitical contexts that shape their daily lives. In a math context, Emma Gargroetzi (as Groetzinger) (2016) describes how producing mathographies allowed young people to reflect on their previous relationships to the discipline of math, feelings toward the subject, and personal experiences in math classrooms. This writing brokered powerful learning opportunities and guided the teacher's instructional decisions moving forward. Having students speak their truths, in a manner that reveals the person they wish to be in your classroom, could be a useful step in your practice.

We have spent significant time at the beginning of each year diving deeply into the norms that will govern the democratic practices of our classrooms. It is possible that norms are deliberately developed in your classroom as well, but if they don't function as clearly understood commitments for all your class members, they may not be playing the fundamental and necessary role that they could be. Likewise, in our experience, norms often require revision and revisiting as a year progresses—both as a reminder of the commitments we hold and to allow students to consider what needs to be edited, added, and removed. Whatever your beginning-of-the-year routines may be, envision what the process of developing class agreements will look like and what they will *feel* like for students (see Figure 3–1).

For us, these are times that we encourage and model for students in a classroom to face one another, literally seeing each other. We ask for and use the names and pronouns our students provide to us and encourage students to do the same for one another. Depending on the context and age group you are teaching, this could be a survey given out at the beginning

FIGURE 3-1 Some examples of opening routines

OPENING ROUTINE	LOOKS LIKE	FEELS LIKE
Post list of rules you have created and discuss them with students, aiming to come to an agreement or consensus.	Top-down list of rules	Resignation and gaslighting
Create discussion prompts for students to discuss what they want their classroom to look like.	Students centering their classroom needs and facing one another	Affirming and deliberate
Place sticky notes and poster paper around the room noting feelings students think their classroom should uphold (e.g., "Joy," "Curiosity," "Safety").	Students responding and contributing at their own pace	Inviting and democratic

of class (or perhaps digitally even before students enter your classroom), a series of icebreaker activities, name placards placed on student desks, or any other easily accessible approach to referring to students by the names and pronouns they prefer. Depending on your schooling context, it is likely that there are students in your class who do not know other students. Too often teachers worry and labor to know all their students' names as soon as possible. However, having students speak to one another and see each other means building similar expectations for them as well.

This Is a Dialogic Process

From a critical perspective, seeing your students also means your students seeing you. Your own vulnerability, uncertainty, and humility must help lead the setting for your classroom. Just as you are working to dismantle monolithic and essentializing narratives others have impressed upon us—via social media, popular culture, and pervasive *lived* experience—you are working to demonstrate to your students the radical possibilities of teaching, of teachers, and the power of your disciplinary subject matter instruction for humanizing purposes.

Often, traditional classrooms are framed as a top-down transactional process, with teachers *giving* students knowledge and affirming student learning. However, the process we are describing means this work needs to go both ways. As teachers, we need to be seen, need to be vulnerable, and need to let our students see ways to affirm all members of our class-room community—including ourselves.

For research on why centering relationships and love works, see Section 2, pages 32–37.

As you build from this recognition, it's OK to ask your students if the interests you *think* they have are accurate, if the uncertainties they feel are the same ones they actually share in your classrooms. Furthermore, as you consider how you get to know your students, keep in mind that you aren't the first teacher to try to care (or just say you care) about your students. Depending on each of their past experiences, students will enter into the classroom you are all building with varying degrees of willingness to open themselves to you and to their classmates. In our experience, students carry deep-seated and valid animosity; classrooms for some have been sites of embarrassment, unreciprocated vulnerability, and pain. We need to lead and show, over time, that ours is a space that trusts young people. This is an ongoing process, and it also isn't acceptable to force students to reveal the vulnerable parts of themselves they may not want to.

As the next section emphasizes what can be done with a classroom designed around trust and recognition, we acknowledge that the feelings of care, vulnerability, and tenderness we describe here may feel radically different from how you were trained or what you expect a classroom and teaching to look like. Part of our task of focusing on tuned-in teaching practice is to reimagine the possibilities of our classrooms. As we move away from classrooms designed in a factory-model vision to join a postindustrial labor force, and toward a brighter possibility of what an education is *for*, we need to rethink our assumptions of classroom life. We ground tuned-in teaching with the selves our students represent and the identities we share with them, because this is where all relationships, innovations, and forms of revolution start. Being tuned-in requires a relational connection, and as a teacher there is an implicit co-participant that you are tuned in with. Let's be frank: there are a lot of

Your own vulnerability, uncertainty, and humility must help lead the setting for your classroom. Just as you are working to dismantle monolithic and essentializing narratives others have impressed upon us—via social media, popular culture, and pervasive lived experience—you are working to demonstrate to your students the radical possibilities of teaching, of teachers, and the power of English language arts instruction for humanizing purposes.

other books you could be reading if you simply wanted to be tuned in to impersonal educational research; we are writing for you to connect with and see the individuals who are in your classroom now.

Action #2: Authenticity as a Standard

Particularly in the moment that we write this, standards convey a specific set of expectations of what has to happen in classrooms. Whether your state and district rely on the Common Core State Standards, a set of district heuristics, or a different set of requirements, standards evoke a set of nonnegotiable requirements on how classroom teaching is enacted. However, when we ruminate on the multiple meanings of the word, *standards* can evoke other kinds of professional engagements with your classroom. From one perspective, standards can be your familiar go-to repertoires in your classroom. Like old jazz and blues chord changes, your standards can be built upon and improvised over time in ways that allow you to flex your practice around familiarity and comfort. Similarly, what is standard is also what is *natural* and *accustomed to*. In this sense, we want you to center authentic forms of engagement as a standard that you push your classroom practice toward.

What do we mean when we say authentic? We think about it in several different ways. Educational researcher Joseph Polman (2012) highlights three different dimensions of authenticity. Focusing on contexts of project-based learning, Polman explains first that instruction should utilize authentic cultural tools—the resources and materials that are valued by specific communities outside of schools (Boardman et al. 2021). In designing instruction, consider the modes of discourse an online fan community engages in, the resources YouTube and TikTok content producers rely upon for producing and uploading content, or whatever other kinds of youth-driven activities occur in your classroom. Second, as mentioned in Section 2, teachers need to center engagement with an authentic community and audience beyond the classroom. Rather than work that is assessed by you as a singular audience or the limited (but still meaningful) interactions with peers, consider how student production can shift when speaking to audiences with different interests, perspectives, and rhetorical approaches. Finally and perhaps most importantly, classrooms must foster authentic personal agency for students such that they feel they are able to make meaningful decisions about topics relevant to their lives. In your classroom how can you make sure of each of the following?

■ Students are presented with a variety of topics to explore.

   ■ A literature class might offer a range of book choices to encourage students to pick from titles that are appealing while still ensuring the books are organized around central instructional goals.

■ Students have space for offering their own interests to the classroom.

   ■ Students might write letters to political candidates related to topics they care about (see Garcia, Levinson, and Gargroetzi 2020).

■ Students can demonstrate expertise in topics that are given meaningful time in your classroom.

   ■ A student who is interested in cars might describe some of the repair work they have done as it relates to thermodynamics.

This feeling of the actions in the classroom leading to feelings of supporting individual agency requires refocusing on the kinds of products that are created and on who decides how they are enacted. As we note later, they require a codesigned approach to instruction.

Authenticity doesn't have to mean reinventing the curricular wheel. It does mean attuning your design work to the interests and knowledge you have of your students. Have your students turned in projects in your classroom that mirror the media they make recreationally, like social media posts, Twitch streams, or Spotify playlists? These examples will change over time and it will require staying abreast to what platforms your students' imaginations frolic upon. Though no unit is ever designed or taught perfectly, you can intentionally design around the three dimensions of authenticity described earlier to better connect to the lives of your students.

Codesigning Engagement

Inventing meaningful and transformative curriculum is both your professional commitment and the great privilege you possess as part of being a teacher. That being said, this work of designing and implementing curriculum that best suits the needs of your students is challenging; make sure others—your administrators, your family, your friends, your students' parents, and your colleagues—recognize the great intellectual and visionary work that our society too often takes for granted. When we describe codesigning here, we mean that every classroom has the potential for student input in most aspects of how the space looks and operates. From the physical layout of the classroom to the kinds of procedures and rules that govern the space, ensuring students can participate in whatever ways naturally suit them in your classroom is an important experience. Furthermore, this great work isn't something that you need to do alone. We *highly* encourage you to collaborate with other teachers, with local organizations and businesses, and with nearby universities to make more meaningful the curricular work you are doing around authenticity. Perhaps most importantly, we encourage you to codesign with your students.

If you've done the work of the previous section in *seeing* and *knowing* your students, it is important for your classroom to reflect and push upon this knowledge and allow this to be an environment for continual growth. This is also considered a perpetual "zone of proximal development" from a Vygotskian perspective of sociocultural learning (Vygotsky 1978). There are five scales with which we think it's best to consider how to have students codesign with you:

1. Across an entire year (or longer): At the end of a school year, having students reflect upon and offer critical feedback on the class allows you to tweak and adjust according to their input.

2. Across a unit: At the end of a unit, consider holding a focus group with students, issuing an open-ended survey, and engaging in a Socratic dialogue to allow students to offer critical advice and guidance for improving your work as a teacher.

3. Across a lesson: Though the previous two scales are often about revising lessons and units for future classes, it is also important to recognize that students are powerful designers within the moment as well. Asking students to consider and to lead lessons based on the expertise that you have learned they have is an important way to center their expertise in the classroom.

4. Within the moment: No lesson is perfect, and you should create an environment where the purpose for a class is clear and students may offer (and you should be ready to solicit ideas for) ways to better execute a specific activity. Perhaps a student imagines a new way of composing, a new set of discussion questions, or a connection within a text that you had not anticipated: these are huge moments for validating youth expertise, getting in touch with students' voices, and learning powerfully new pedagogical lessons from a new generation.

5. As the real-world dictates: Though you may have important lessons that you have poured your soul into, sometimes the outside world requires a break in your lesson plan. Whether a national disaster, an election, a local news event, or a school-based situation is at the heart, the interests and uncertainties of our students require our classrooms to be places to make meaning of the outside world. This often means unexpectedly but necessarily having to switch to a new curricular design.

When we codesign with our students and when we engage in authentic learning practices tied to audiences and interests beyond rote, "traditional" standards, we take powerful steps toward redefining classrooms. These become spaces that slowly de-center adults as singular authoritative voices in classrooms and instead mirror a public sphere in which democratic ideas and synergistic work are enacted for powerful purposes.

Focusing on #4 and #5, it is hard to get students to codesign with you if you don't trust them in their wisdom or create an environment where they can freely voice their ideas. Furthermore, if you don't *know* your students, how will you be able to draw upon their knowledge as you design work? When I, Antero, was still in the classroom, I had one student who was a passionate novelist, and I recruited her help in leading creative writing lessons in conjunction with the annual National Novel Writing Month competition held internationally each November. That student helped drive what happened in the classroom, cocreated a powerful learning model for her classmates, and (perhaps tellingly) is an English teacher in her own classroom today.

When we codesign with our students and when we engage in authentic learning practices tied to audiences and interests beyond rote, "traditional" standards, we take powerful steps toward redefining classrooms. These become spaces that slowly de-center adults as singular authoritative voices in classrooms and instead mirror a public sphere in which democratic ideas and synergistic work are enacted for powerful purposes.

Action #3: Get in Touch with Students' Digital Lives

For most of us, the resources in classrooms that we teach students with today look vastly different from what they looked like in the past. The projectors are connected to computers that are connected to the internet and the rest of the world, pens and pencils are often replaced with tablets and laptops, and homework posted on the board is sent electronically to students through personalized learning systems or—if a student is in a hurry—perhaps captured through a snapshot on a mobile device.

Despite the dizzying shifts in technology that have arrived in the professional and personal lives of students and adults alike, classrooms still tend to operate in the same factory model that has persisted for generations. While the rest of the world is dealing with labor challenges tied to automation, algorithms, and globalization, classrooms must move toward better reflecting the digital needs of students once they leave classrooms. As we offer several approaches next, we first acknowledge three things:

1. The use of technology in your classroom is not a panacea for addressing educational inequities or capturing the interests of all your students.

2. Investing time in studying and utilizing singular tools will not prepare students for navigating the broader world of digital and analog media production and consumption that awaits them.

3. Ignoring digital tools does not meaningfully help students prepare for their future outside of school.

As a key first step to powerful instruction that utilizes technology, building from these three tenets is tantamount. If your teaching feels out of touch, an app or digital tool ain't gonna fix it. Instead, it is important to look at the world outside of schools and mirror how technology mediates interactions, learning, and labor. This isn't as lofty as it sounds; it can start with a reflection on your own relationship with technology. If you're at all like us, your mobile device might buzz periodically throughout the day as friends, family, and colleagues communicate with you. And—if you're like us—you might send a quick reply or check a status notification on your phone *even* while you're on the job. This isn't something to feel guilty about (though if your relationship to work means responding to emails and texts at all hours of the day, a more mindful approach to media use is worth considering!). Instead, we highlight that many middle-class and upper-class jobs encourage such frequent communication and offer the freedom and *trust* in employees to take their social behavior into their own hands (literally).

Teaching your content area within continually changing, digitally mediated environments can feel dizzying for us as teachers. Instead of trying to stay up-to-date with the increasingly expensive world of educational technology, being mindful and present of how media is utilized in your own world and that of your friends and colleagues is a more useful starting place. In writing about the valuable role of in-touch technology use in classrooms, Antero and our colleague Thomas Philip urge educators to emphasize the "context" rather than the "tools" for learning. By this we mean that the ecosystem in which technology plays a part in our lives is an important one for teachers and students to intentionally consider as we write, produce, and communicate. Like we mentioned above, it's OK that you are looking at and occasionally using your mobile device during school hours. At the same time, maybe your classroom can be a place where students are able to more intentionally consider their relationships to technology. As an actionable step, consider how your classroom learning goals are going to use technology and—if you have activities that *can* be broadened through connections to social media and to online resources and opportunities for creative expression with digital tools—intentionally design and teach in ways to highlight these possibilities. For example, some classrooms we have worked with create a classroom-designated Twitter account to share student ideas publicly while also protecting student anonymity. Perhaps consider using education-focused online resources, like KQED's Learn platform, that allow students to safely communicate and explore in spaces that develop powerful media literacy skills.

Finally, as a caveat, we acknowledge that discussing student-owned technology like mobile phones can create a lot of anxiety and frustration for teachers: these devices can often distract and impede our learning expectations. However, perhaps it is because our school policies are out of touch with the rest of the world. Though it may seem beyond the scope of this book, we do think it may be time for educators and students alike to reconsider the role of technology and how power and authority are enacted in classrooms. Creating tuned-in teaching contexts means reimagining the possibilities of our classrooms, and this includes the tools available at our collective fingertips.

> For research on digital literacies and youth popular culture, see Section 2, pages 22–27.

Enacting Critical Media Pedagogies

In a talk at the 2018 South by Southwest conference, media researcher danah boyd described how previous teaching approaches to media literacy have backfired. Pointing to invocations of "fake news" and to the echo chamber effect that limit dialogue within the United States, boyd's talk emphasizes that the key contexts of media literacy, such as questioning and seeking multiple perspectives, have reinforced hateful messages and caused symbolic and literal harm. This is particularly true for marginalized and vulnerable communities. As she wrapped up her talk after examples of violence, democratic threat, and meme culture, boyd confessed that she didn't have immediate answers as to what teachers can do. Clearly, traditional models of media literacy have confined specific forms of analysis that have not effectively improved the social fabric, particularly if we are looking at online discourse on spaces like Facebook and Twitter.

Though boyd's talk illustrates that the field of media literacy is currently in a key moment of transformation and interrogation, we do think there are some important considerations that you can engage with in your classroom right away. As Thoman and Jolls (2005) have suggested, engaging in questions with students that look less at *how* messages are constructed and more at the values implied within them is an important beginning step. Asking what values are represented (and omitted) within a text is an important topic that you can engage with students of all ages and *any* subject. Rather than beginning with an abstract, holistic look at how digital texts are produced, dig deep into the values that students see within a text and whom it views as its intended audience.

Together and with other teachers and researchers, we have written extensively about engaging with and teaching media *critically* (Garcia 2017; Garcia, Seglem, and Share 2013; Morrell 2006; Morrell et al. 2013). As we urge your work in classrooms to better connect with the media lives of young people, we encourage you to engage in class discussions and reflections about the media that students not only consume but that they also produce. From TikTok to Instagram to text messages with friends and family, students are *always* creating complicated and multimodal products. Although they may not want their teachers to be privy to the content of these messages, allowing students to demonstrate their work as producers and their knowledge about the genre conventions of these different spaces can be important ways to affirm student learning.

Don't Get Swept Up by the Digital Wave

Finally, we encourage you to not worry so much about technology. There's a lot of world for your students to study, explore, and imagine even without Wi-Fi. Although there continues to be an interest in twenty-first-century learning that is tied to global communication and amplification, the answers to be a more tuned-in teacher aren't to be found in digital tools. Instead, facing your students in the analog settings of our classrooms (Garcia 2020), building face-to-face relationships, and cultivating an uncompressed, non-digitized ethos of love is going to ultimately transform students' lives. We write this not to diminish the possibilities of technology but rather to let you know it's OK not to sweat knowing the ins and outs of the latest iGadget; knowing your students, your content area, and the possibilities of radical imagination are more than enough to get started. Many years ago, in my, Antero's, classroom, I built a student-dedicated MySpace page for students to communicate and reach out around expectations in their classroom (years later this would become a Facebook page). I didn't necessarily know how to effectively use this tool, but it meant students helped me and it became a space where they were familiar and willing to reach out in ways that they might not have in the regular, physical classroom.

Action #4: Keep It Playful

When we imagine the world that we want students to eventually lead, live, and thrive in, there is an abundance of big tasks that need to be accomplished. Systemic inequities that plague our society have gone unaddressed for generations. The students in our classroom will inherit the necessary and urgent task of working to better the conditions for historically marginalized individuals around the globe on top of fitting into the ever-shifting contexts of a globalized, capitalist society. Labor, passion, and justice are *heavy* topics, and the gravitas of what we do in our classrooms on a day-to-day basis is important. We should take seriously our task as teachers. That being said, we emphasize that our students must also have opportunities to play, to be wildly imaginative, and to laugh. As you work to improve your classroom instruction, look over your plans and intentionally consider:

- How often is laughter cultivated in your class on a daily basis?

- When are students provided opportunities to play, strategize, and consider learning from a game-based perspective?

- What kinds of imaginative tasks are taken up in students' reading, writing, and communication?

Enthusiasm and levity are important; this speaks to seeing the full humanity of the students in your classroom, as we discussed in Section 2. Getting tuned in with effective teaching for students requires remembering that a joyful life can be cultivated in our classrooms. Just because the work we do is important does not mean that it cannot be fun—as teachers we consistently hope that students will enter into work around something they are passionate about. In our classrooms, we can create opportunities for levity, show our smiling humanity, and demonstrate our own enthusiasm for our curriculum to affirm this side of civic life to our students. Depending on your context, this could mean exploring political humor on shows like *Saturday Night Live*, or perhaps remixing classroom content in ways that create parody and jokes shared by your students.

Furthermore, games and play are an important way for students to understand complex systems and situations that may shape their experiences beyond the real world. There are existing games that can be quickly utilized in your classroom for specific kinds of learning outcomes and ways to remix or "hack" games for specific goals. Educator Allan Johnson (2001), for example, has highlighted simple modifications to the game of Monopoly to teach about systemic inequality. As a game initially meant to critique systems of capitalism, Monopoly plays a unique role in popular culture today: it has sold millions of copies, nearly everyone in the United States knows the basic rules of the game, and (at least in our experience) most people don't actually like the game that much! As a game that is easy to acquire, it is a great opportunity to explore a myriad of issues and to improve a game play experience that most people find mundane. Likewise, even social games like Werewolf, Apples to Apples, and Game of Phones allow students to communicate with their peers, collaborate, and smile in ways that traditional curriculum often gets in the way of. Playing in classrooms provides opportunities for students to socialize in new ways and potentially connect games to content-focused curriculum. Games can frequently offer a systems-focused perspective of how mechanisms like inequality operate throughout society. And they might just make in-touch teaching feel more fun.

Labor, passion, and justice are heavy topics, and the gravitas of what we do in our classrooms on a day-to-day basis is important. We should take seriously our task as teachers. That being said, we emphasize that our students must also have opportunities to play, to be wildly imaginative, and to laugh.

Playing Toward Justice

Creating opportunities for play and imagination in classrooms is also an issue of justice. If we consider the increased surveillance, criminalization, and adultization of Black and brown youth in communities today, the freedoms to explore and to be imaginative are cast as suspicious.

They are the policies that led to fourteen-year-old Ahmed Mohammed being handcuffed for bringing a homemade clock to school in 2015. Likewise, as schools frequently focus on test prep, opportunities for arts-based expression, learning, and exploration are being diminished. Current policies around safety in urban communities and around high-stakes, for-profit testing mean that play is relegated to the bottom of the priorities for students. At the same time, daydreaming, wild ideation, and rapid prototype development are the attributes of white entrepreneurial visionaries from Albert Einstein to Walt Disney to Steve Jobs (and not Katherine Johnson, David Ho, and Jodi Muñoz).

Similarly, when we think about approaches that engage students, we don't mean that you can simply throw out traditional texts or content to appear authentically interested in the needs and interests of your students. Imagination and literature go hand in hand. In English classrooms, for example, revitalizing the inspiring possibilities of the work of Shakespeare, of Toni Morrison, and of your own students is one of the most exciting aspects of our profession. In fact, perhaps literature can play an even *more* important role in the lives of young people than before. We recognize that many district- and statewide policies emphasize informational texts as a focus in classrooms. We believe that informational texts are a huge component of how teachers (in all subject areas) can work toward justice in their tuned-in classrooms. There are plenty of *good* informational texts available to teachers, and these fit in well with project-based learning work that may be justice-oriented. At the same time, we consider how literature and storytelling have the power to spark imagination, to heal, and to guide new ways of imaging the world around us. In speaking to literature that has specific activist possibilities, adrienne maree brown and Walidah Imarisha (2016) describe the authoring of "visionary fiction" as "the work of people who use fiction to advance justice and liberation" (27).

From Afrofuturist authors like Octavia Butler to canonical authors like Plato and postcolonial novelists such as Gabriel Garcia Marquez, the possibilities of fiction to point to future worlds and societies is an intentional aspect of texts in your classroom that can help students see novels as blueprints for rebuilding a new social order (e.g., Counts 1932). History teachers might look to the blueprints of such imaginative authors to consider how historical efforts related to societies and utopias fit with these futuristic visions. Likewise, an accounting of the logistics of launching and operating new forms of settlement and shared living—in new locations or alternate planets—could become a broad project-based learning topic that includes issues of economics, science, statistics, algebra, and English language arts.

Ultimately making your classroom a center of joy in the lives of your students and a place for playfulness may feel trite and secondary (or tertiary) to the many, many demands on your time as a teacher. However, in our experience designing around the needs for play, imagination and levity are often joyful processes, in and of themselves, and further engaging in intellectual joyfulness can feel synergistic (e.g., Dalai Lama and Tutu (Bstan 2016). Moving from spelling out for students "This is how the world works" to having students question "*What if* the world worked like this?" is an agentic opportunity we hope you will play with in your instructional design.

Action #5: Center Action

Implicit throughout the actions we've listed so far is the fact that learning in powerful tuned-in classrooms is intentionally *active* and action-oriented. Though interrelated with the other actions noted previously, we describe the specific principles of active classrooms here. In calling for your classroom to center action, we mean that learning, writing, and production should be tied to specific, actionable, and authentic goals (and by *authentic* we mean the multidimensional description we discussed earlier in this chapter). Active classrooms will require a variety of different roles for students, shifts in leadership, and potentially different physical arrangements of the classroom, its bodies, and its furniture. However, before making intentional decisions about each of these aspects of action-centered instruction, you and your students must come to a common understanding about what action you are undertaking and for what kinds of projected outcomes. In this sense, we suggest a Goldilocks-like approach to centering action in your classroom: you do not want to take on issues so broad that your classroom feels like it is throwing an inconsequential snowball at the sun, nor do you want to address a topic that feels so inconsequential that students' actions feel minuscule.

The actions of your classrooms will feel *just right* when they take up the multiple meanings of those two words. On the one hand, the action is just "right" because it is of a manageable size; perhaps your students take up an action research project studying dropout statistics for your school or district to publish student-centered op-eds and present their findings to the local school board, for example. At the same time, such a topic is "just" as it arises *just in time*: What topics do your students and you feel are urgent, are provoking emotional, logical, and ethical discussions within your community? Furthermore, just as history has borne out nuanced interpretations of right and wrong, a cursory look at civil rights movements finds that actions that are just right tend to align with the views, dignities, and fought-for rights of historically marginalized communities. A just-right action is one that defines a specific kind of justice by your students and works to more closely tilt the world in that direction.

> *The actions of your classrooms will feel* just right *when they take up the multiple meanings of those two words.*

Getting to decide upon an action, the logic of a collective theory of change around it, and the intellectual roots that will be required, demands that you both know and trust your students as committed colleagues in a vision of action. Furthermore, we recognize that students are not a singular entity: your classroom is filled with *individuals*, and their sense of the world and their role within it will vary. This may mean working toward several different kinds of actions. As long as these are interwoven toward collective social justice, we encourage you to find ways to be flexible and nimble when designing to the actions that spur enthusiasm within your classroom. As described in Section 2, a Youth Participatory Action Research approach might inspire students to take up varied research topics and explore them

For research on Youth Participatory Action Research, see Section 2, pages 27–32.

in different ways. For example, in my, Antero's, classroom, students identified topics around their school that they wanted to investigate, including "the absence of love" in South Central Los Angeles, the poor quality of the school's food, and the lack of healthy eating options near the school. Students documented their questions with photos, interviews, and historical research before developing a playful set of findings that led to a daylong on-campus scavenger hunt (this full project is described in Garcia [2017]).

Reading as Action

We recognize that the descriptions of action and activism in this section may feel very different from what you might imagine a typical classroom looks like. On the one hand, the structures of schooling—physical and symbolic—have been long established to orient student bodies and identities in ways that suppress their collective voices and power. The orientation of desks, the factory-like adherence to bells, and the often-amplified voices of adults over loudspeakers or speaking authoritatively from the front of classrooms are all aspects of schools that identify, historically, the subservient role of students. At the same time, you might imagine aspects of your classroom as critical and liberatory, aligned with the vision of justice this action describes. In our own practice, we fondly remember the aspects of teaching a class novel and discussing passionately aspects of works from across a diverse and historically important canon of authors. Whether it was looking at ideas of agency, free will, and resistance in the works of Shakespeare or considering aspects of identity, systemic inequality, and feminism in the works of Toni Morrison, our identities as enthusiastic readers played large parts in what teaching were about.

To this end, we wish to clear the air a bit: though we do believe that your classroom must work to operate in opposition to many of the existing structural aspects of schools that deny youth voices, we also feel that teaching toward action includes important pedagogical decisions, and your expertise as an educator should always guide how content is explored. Similarly in this vein, we intentionally dispel the notion that reading is a passive act. As an active process for synthesizing ideas and building new knowledge, literature can act as a bedrock for rebuilding a collective social imagination. Even as your students may engage in multimodal research or action that includes film, tweets, augmented reality, and whatever other tools permeate your classroom, the role of novels in guiding particular ontological understandings of the world, of society, and of us as individuals remains an important aspect of what happens in your classroom. This does mean you should be intentional with which texts you introduce to your students and for what purpose: *Why* are you assigning the novel or informational texts? What do these texts enable?

Finally, as your classroom grows around powerfully integrating reading as an active source of learning, we recognize that reading in all subject areas can look very different from what is traditionally assumed. Reading can include a vast variety of multimodal texts that are read, swiped, and interacted with in different genres and different languages. Furthermore, as we consider the proliferation of podcasts and audiobooks easily downloadable onto smartphones and mobile media devices today, the possibilities of *listening* as a form of reading must also be acknowledged (Garcia 2017).

The Courage of Action

This action—and several others thus far—allude to activism as a formative possibility for learning in your classroom. We first note that an action-oriented classroom is not the same as an activist classroom (though they could share similarities). Though we affirm classroom practices that specifically work to fight oppression at all levels, teachers might feel more comfortable starting by focusing on classrooms that have students engaging in work that moves outside of the classroom—to public audiences—and allows students to voice their thinking in new ways. However, we also want to be clear that the public schools in which most teachers work today are not neutral spaces. The politics of schooling—both in the United States and internationally—have shaped the lasting legacies of inequality that we must collectively work toward mending (e.g., Tyack and Cuban 1995; Willis 1977). Reform takes both action and activism. Building a curriculum that actively improves the world requires courage, creativity, and collaboration with the students you are entrusted to work with.

> *Reform takes both action and activism. Building a curriculum that actively improves the world requires courage, creativity, and collaboration with the students you are entrusted to work with.*

Action #6: Put It All Together

As important as each of the actions described thus far are in furthering the powerful learning opportunities in your classroom, in this final section we want to help you consider how these different aspects of pedagogy work together synergistically. Admittedly, this is a challenging ask, and we have placed it near the end of this book to recognize that you may spend parts of your career more intentionally addressing some of the actions noted above over others. You are probably already excelling at some of these before even opening this book! However, to most fully take advantage of the concepts we've discussed throughout this text, we offer a generative sense of how these pieces interlock, acknowledge the assumptions of knowledge as it's produced in classrooms, and—as is increasingly important in today's educational landscape—discuss the role of assessment across these actions. We begin by digging into the implicit epistemological stance of the ideas we've presented.

Episte-what?

Though not the most common or familiar word in classroom and professional development texts, *epistemology* is a foundational component of how we educate teachers and students alike. Loosely, an epistemology describes one's theory of knowledge; how do we know what we know is a key question that an epistemology attempts to describe. The implicit ways that we learn about the world, about society, and about ourselves are built into nearly every lesson and interaction we have with students. And yet, aside from discussing varied theories of pedagogical skills for youth acquisition of knowledge, the epistemological foundations of our work are not discussed.

Just as we think it is important for teachers to make knowledgeable decisions about what and how they teach, we also feel it is important to explain the theory of what knowledge *is* and how it is formed throughout the actions we've described in this chapter. In this sense, the activities across this book highlight that knowledge is not finite in its nature. There is an abundance of knowledge being constantly produced, circulated, and built upon. Looking at your classroom as a site for generating knowledge and sharing new ideas reshapes expertise for both teachers and students. Though some important aspects of commonly held and critical knowledge can be excavated from texts and databases in our classrooms, so too can new knowledge be developed, understood, defended, and upheld daily by you and by your students.

Epistemologically, each of the actions we describe center building and interpreting new and relevant knowledge in classrooms. This means challenging commonly held assumptions of expertise, building on the interests of students, and remaining in dialogue with the world that exists beyond the walls of the school.

A Note on Assessment

Typically, a key consideration of how curriculum is designed and implemented in classrooms is the role of assessment. What will be assessed, how often, by which means, and for what purposes? With the vision of a generative, responsive classroom that we present here, the role of assessment remains no less important. Done well, an assessment allows teachers to make informed, customized decisions about the needs of their students and their class. In this sense, we see the role of formative assessments—given frequently and in myriad supportive forms—as critical in understanding where your students are headed, what they are struggling with, and how to best tailor support for them as individuals. The NCTE Task Force on Assessment (2013) has provided useful guidelines for designing and considering the role of formative assessment.

At the same time that we see assessment as critical for student progress, we are also aware of how the current sociopolitical climate of schooling has made overtesting a taxing aspect of many students' lives and a stressful aspect of how too many teachers are evaluated today. This aspect of assessment—the measurement of disembodied knowledge not tethered to meaningful outcomes for students—is not imperative to our vision of tuned-in teaching. However, we also recognize that your context and the demands on you as a member of the teaching profession in your particular district may mean adjusting your classroom practice to fit in assessments that you may not ideologically agree with and that may speak to other epistemological traditions that are not tuned in to the cultural needs and values of you or your students. The flexibility to accommodate such demands, the transparency of *why* these exist as an opportunity for student reflection, and the ability to quickly move from these out-of-touch assessments to the more organic forms of knowledge will highlight your ability to synthesize powerful pedagogical models.

These Actions Are Not Definitive

Finally, as we encourage you to put these actions together into a powerful, flexible, and responsive classroom pedagogy, we also recognize that we have not offered a fully comprehensive roll call of the actions that are required of you in your day-to-day commitment as a growing teacher. We are not qualified to do so. Each of our classrooms changes from one moment to the next. The needs of the students in your classroom tomorrow, next year, or next decade will be substantial and unprecedented. We don't assume that we have the cure-all solution for in-touch teaching for the foreseeable future. That being said, we have made these actions flexible and customizable for your practice. As much as we cannot predict where the world is headed (that's in the hands of our students!), we do believe that the interconnected actions presented here are a starting place for growing and continually learning alongside the students in our classrooms. In Figure 3–2, we return to all six of the principles in this section with some starting prompts for your ideas to take flight.

FIGURE 3-2 Tuned-In teaching approaches

PRINCIPLES	QUESTIONS	SUGGESTIONS
1. Students at the Center	How are you ensuring you are fully seeing who your students are? What do student values mean in how you teach every day?	Create routines that affirm student identities. Allow yourself to be a vulnerable member of your classroom community.
2. Authenticity as a Standard	How do student interests and expertise get to shine within your classroom? What aspects of your teaching practice are you willing to negotiate and cede to student ideas and ingenuity?	Ensure that some activities in your classroom are open-ended for students to choose the topics they will explore. Consider where students might codesign elements of your classroom.
3. Get in Touch with Students' Digital Lives	When does technology get in the way of your teaching goals? Are there areas of student uses of technology that could be meaningfully incorporated into your classroom?	Before jumping to the next digital tool, consider what relationships and practices you want to cultivate and how digital culture might support these practices. Include opportunities for students to engage in digital media *production* in addition to critiquing and exploring texts that are consumed for academic learning.
4. Keep It Playful	How is student curiosity cultivated in your classroom? Humor is culturally dependent. How are you ensuring that what feels playful to you is also playful to your students?	Don't be afraid to have fun in your classroom. Incorporate texts and resources that are humorous and may add levity to your classroom.

(continues)

(continued)

5. Center Action	Who are the audiences your students communicate with? What texts inspire you and might inspire your students? How can you incorporate them?	Consider local organizations and families that might help expand the reach of your classroom. Find ways to integrate meaningful literature and informational texts throughout your instructional plans.
6. Put It All Together	How do you assess learning in your classroom? There are a *lot* of ideas in this section. What one or two things might you want to start with?	Give assessments components that are meaningful beyond purely evaluating academic growth (e.g., does the work further movements for justice, spark intrigue in its intended audience, reach new audiences?). Find aspects of what feels out-of-touch in your own classroom context and transform it!

Conclusion

Throughout this section, we have offered a half dozen approaches to bringing your classroom more meaningfully to the needs of your students, your community, and the broader world. In the previous parts of this book, we've detailed works to challenge the out-of-touch teaching practices that bore and infantilize our students while also undermining the expertise of the teaching profession. As we conclude this book, we consider what *out of touch* means and—in particular—for whom. Many classrooms *can* be deeply tuned in with the academic progress that the state may require that students attain, while also feeling out of touch with the lives and interests of students. However, even in working to prepare students through drill-and-kill test prep, these classrooms are often out of touch with the other aspects of students' lives.

Similar to other questions we've asked throughout this book, we encourage you to reflect broadly on the role of instruction and relationships in your classrooms: when considering what is *tuned-in* about your practice, question *for whom* and *for why*? Putting names and faces to the need for specific kinds of instructional designs means looking broadly at the world you are preparing your students for and drawing a straight line between your instructional intent and the kinds of civic, social, and emotional individuals you are attempting to support. This vision of learning is inherently holistic and must take up not only the often taken-for-granted role of academic learning but also the sociocultural values of students, the technological advances of the world, the political and socioeconomic shifts that affect life globally and locally, and the civic needs for students to literally change the world. These are, obviously, very *big* considerations to make, and they highlight the shifts in your practice and the teaching culture this book works to guide. They speak to making yours a more culturally relevant and proactive environment for students and teachers alike.

Finally, as we've made clear throughout this book, we are not alone in working toward a more human vision of schooling and of the relationships forged within classrooms. This work is built on generations of individuals contributing thoughtful scholarship, mentorship, and pedagogical innovation. Too, it is built on the ingenuity and joy and insights young people have shared with us in schools. Furthermore, critical research is the lodestone that guides decisions we make in our classrooms and in the pathways we help tread toward tuned-in teaching practices. The large bodies of work on culturally responsive instruction that also build on including youth popular culture within your classrooms have served as a foundation for this work. At the same time, even lengthier inquiries into cultural studies, sociocultural literacies, and critical theory explore the relationships between labor and power. Furthermore, organizers across generations that fight for the civil rights of all play a central role in the whys and hows of in-touch teaching practices. Through learning from and standing upon the shoulders of these intellectual and civic giants, we are excited for your classroom to flourish.

AFTERWORD

Nell K. Duke

*M*any readers of this book are familiar with the concept of a professional learning community or PLC. EdGlossary defines a PLC as "a group of educators that meets regularly, shares expertise, and works collaboratively to improve teaching skills and the academic performance of students." A wide range of activities occur under the banner of a PLC, among them examining student assessment data, reading books and articles selected by participants, and sharing instructional strategies.

A cousin of the PLC is a teacher study group or TSG. In a recent article, Allison Firestone, Rebecca Cruz, and Janelle Rodl (2020) reviewed research on TSGs, finding that they are a promising approach to fostering teacher development and student achievement. TSGs are similar to PLCs in that they are collaborative groups of educators who meet on a regular basis to engage in inquiry regarding their teaching and their students' learning. However, TSGs differ from PLCs in that "they are predicated upon a preplanned scope and sequence and content grounded in empirical research . . . by design, a TSG includes the provision of new content in order to increase collective knowledge by leveraging some form of expert input (e.g., a university faculty member or master teacher) to facilitate integration of new knowledge and skills into the inquiry process" (677). In other words, TSGs value both knowledge from teacher participants and knowledge from external expertise, often in the form of research.

In this remarkable book, Antero Garcia and Ernest Morrell highlight that there is a third source of knowledge that must be central in teacher development—students themselves. Garcia and Morrell help us to understand the importance of learning about the students in front of us: their cultural backgrounds, their identities, their interests, their digital lives, their ideas, their expertise, their humor and play, their families, and the organizations in their communities that affect and are affected by them. Learning about the students in front of us on an ongoing basis—being *in touch* with them—renders teaching more effective and more humanizing.

In a way, then, every day with students is an opportunity for professional development, in which the professional development providers are students themselves. PLCs or TSGs become an opportunity in part to process what is learned from students, to work with colleagues to build collective understandings (for example, of digital literacies popular with students), and to integrate what is learned from students with learnings from research and practice.

Like any form of professional learning, professional learning from and with students will not be easy. As Garcia and Morrell note, "No teacher aspires to foster an out-of-touch teaching practice," yet it is all too easy to teach in a way that is uninformed or underinformed by the students in front of us. Even with a deep understanding of our students, there will be challenges in integrating and acting upon what we learn. For example, Garcia and Morrell probe, "What aspects of your teaching practice are you willing to negotiate and cede to student ideas and ingenuity?" But meeting these challenges will be well worth it. In fact perhaps my favorite aspect of this book is the ways in which the authors steel us against challenges and inspire us to action and improvement. Whether in a PLC or TSG, let's tune in to our students ASAP.

REFERENCES

Adelman, Clem. 1993. "Kurt Lewin and the Origins of Action Research." *Educational Action Research* 1 (1): 7–24.

Adorno, Theodor W., and Mark Horkheimer. 1944. "The Culture Industry: Enlightenment as Mass Deception." In *Media and Cultural Studies: Keyworks* (2nd ed.), edited by M. G. Durham and D. Kellner, 2001, 53–75. Malden, MA: Blackwell, 2001.

Alim, H. Samy. 2006. *Roc the Mic Right: The Language of Hip Hop Culture*. New York: Routledge.

Allyn, Pam, and Ernest Morrell. 2016. *Every Child a Super Reader: 7 Strengths to Open a World of Possible*. New York: Scholastic.

Anyon, Jean 1981. "Social Class and School Knowledge." *Curriculum Inquiry* 11(1): 3–42. https://doi.org/10 .2307/1179509.

Banks, James A., ed. 1996. *Multicultural Education, Transformative Knowledge, and Action: Historical and Contemporary Perspectives*. New York: Teachers College Press.

Bartolomé, Lilia. 1994. "Beyond the Methods Fetish: Toward a Humanizing Pedagogy." *Harvard Educational Review* 64 (2): 173–95.

Baudrillard, Jean. 2001. *Impossible Exchange*. New York: Verso.

Bautista, Mark, Melanie Bertrand, Ernest Morrell, D'Artagnan Scorza, and Corey Matthews. 2013. "Participatory Action Research and City Youth: Methodological Insights from the Council of Youth Research." *Teachers College Record* 115: 1–23.

Bell, D. A. 1992. *Faces at the Bottom of the Well: The Permanence of Racism.* New York: Basic Books.

Benjamin, Walter. 1935. "The Work of Art in the Age of Mechanical Reproduction." In *Illuminations*, edited by Hannah Arendt, 166–195. New York: Stocken Books, 1969.

Block, Meghan K., and Stephanie L. Strachan. 2019. "The Impact of External Audience on Second Graders' Writing Quality." *Reading Horizons: A Journal of Literacy and Language Arts* 58 (2).

Boardman, Alison, Antero Garcia, Bridget Dalton, & Joseph Polman. 2021. *Compose Our World: Engaging Educators and Students with Project-Based Learning in Secondary English Language Arts.* New York: Teachers College Press.

Bourdieu, Pierre. 1986. "The Forms of Capital." In *Handbook of Theory and Research for the Sociology of Education*, edited by J. Richardson, 241–58. New York: Greenwood.

Bstan-'dzin-rgya-mtsho, 1935– and Desmond Tutu, *The Book of Joy: Lasting Happiness in a Changing World.* New York: Avery, 2016.

Camangian, Patrick. 2010. "Starting with Self: Teaching Autoethnography to Foster Critically Caring Literacies." *Research in the Teaching of English* 45 (2):179–204.

Cammarota, Julie, and Michelle Fine, eds. 2008. *Revolutionizing Education: Youth Participatory Action Research in Motion.* New York: Routledge.

Campano, Gerald. 2007. *Immigrant Students and Literacy: Reading, Writing and Remembering.* New York: Teachers College Press.

Canagarajah, Suresh A. 1999. *Resisting Linguistic Imperialism in English Teaching.* Oxford, England: Oxford University Press.

Caraballo, Limarys, Brian Lozenski, Jamila J. LyisCott, and Ernest Morrell. 2017. "Youth Participatory Action Research and Critical Epistemologies: Rethinking Educational Research." *Review of Research in Education* 41 (1): 311–36.

Chabot, Sean. 2008. "Love and revolution." *Critical Sociology* 34 (6): 803–28.

Chomsky, Noam. 1957. *Syntactic Structures.* Cambridge, MA: MIT Press.

Counts, George S. 1932. *Dare the School Build a New Social Order?* New York: John Day Company.

de los Ríos, Cati V., and Kate Seltzer. 2017. "Translanguaging, Coloniality, and English Classrooms: An Exploration of Two Bicoastal Urban Classrooms." *Research in the Teaching of English* 52 (1): 55–76.

Dewey, John. 1902. *The School and Society; The Child and the Curriculum.* Chicago, IL: The University of Chicago Press.

Duke, Nell K. 2000. "For the Rich It's Richer: Print Experiences and Environments Offered to Children in Very Low- and Very High-Socioeconomic Status First-Grade Classrooms." *American Educational Research Journal* 37 (2): 441–78.

Duncan-Andrade, Jeffrey M. R. 2006. "Research and Urban Education: Utilizing Carino in the Development of Research Methodologies." In *The Praeger Handbook of Urban Education*, edited by Joe Kincheloe, Kecia Hayes, Karel Rose, Philip M. Anderson, 451–60. Westport, CT: Greenwood Press.

———. 2010. *What a Coach Can Teach a Teacher: Lessons Urban Schools Can Learn from a Successful Sports Program.* New York: Peter Lang.

Duncan-Andrade, Jeffrey M. R., and Ernest Morrell. 2008. *The Art of Critical Pedagogy: Possibilities for Moving from Theory to Practice in Urban Schools.* New York: Peter Lang.

EdGlossary. 2014. Professional learning community. March 3. https://www.edglossary.org/professional-learning -community/.

Emdin, Christopher. 2016. *For White Folks Who Teach in the Hood . . . and the Rest of Y'all Too: Reality Pedagogy and Urban Education.* Boston: Beacon.

Erickson, Ansley T., and Ernest Morrell, eds. 2020. *Educating Harlem: A Century of Schooling and Resistance in a Black Community*. New York: Columbia University Press.

Firestone, A. R., R. A. Cruz, and J. E. Rodl. 2020. "Teacher Study Groups: An Integrative Literature Synthesis." *Review of Educational Research* 90 (5): 675–709. https://doi.org/10.3102/0034654320938128.

Fisher, Maisha T. 2007. *Writing in Rhythm: Spoken Word Poetry in Urban Classrooms*. New York: Teachers College Press.

Freire, Paulo. 1970. *Pedagogy of the Oppressed*. New York: Bloomsbury Publishing.

Freire, Paulo, and Donaldo Macedo. 1987. *Literacy: Reading the Word and the World*. Westport, CT: Praeger.

Garcia, Antero. 2017. *Good Reception: Teens, Teachers, and Mobile Media in a Los Angeles High School*. Cambridge, MA: MIT Press.

———. 2020. "Gaming Literacies: Spatiality, Materiality, and Analog Learning in a Digital Age." *Reading Research Quarterly* 55 (1): 9–27.

Garcia, Antero, Amber M. Levinson, and Emma C. Gargroetzi. 2020. "'Dear Future President of the United States': Analyzing Youth Civic Writing Within the 2016 Letters to the Next President Project." *American Educational Research Journal* 57 (3): 1159–1201.

Garcia, Antero, and Cindy O'Donnell-Allen. 2015. *Pose, Wobble, Flow: A Culturally Proactive Approach to Literacy Instruction*. New York: Teachers College Press.

Garcia, Antero, Robyn Seglem, and Jeff Share. 2013. "Transforming Teaching and Learning Through Critical Media Literacy Pedagogy." *Learning Landscapes* 6 (2): 109–23.

García, Ofelia. 2009. *Bilingual Education in the 21st Century: A Global Perspective*. Malden, MA: Wiley-Blackwell.

García, Ofelia, Susana I. Johnson, and Kate Seltzer. 2017. *The Translanguaging Classroom: Leveraging Student Bilingualism for Learning*. Philadelphia: Carlson.

García, Ofelia, and Li Wei. 2014. *Translanguaging: Language, Bilingualism, and Education*. New York: Palgrave MacMillan.

Gee, James P. 2003. *What Video Games Have to Teach Us About Learning and Literacy*. New York: Palgrave Macmillan.

Gould, Carol C. 1978. *Marx's Social Ontology: Individuality and Community in Marx's Theory of Social Reality*. Cambridge, MA: MIT Press.

Gramsci, Antonio. 1971. *Selections from the Prison Notebooks*. New York: International Publishers.

Groetzinger, Emma. 2016. "Mathographies for Equity: Bringing Student Stories into the Classroom." *New England Mathematics Journal* 48 (1): 17–27.

Gutierrez, Kris D. 2008. "Developing a Sociocritical Literacy in the Third Space." *Reading Research Quarterly* 43 (2): 148–64.

Howard, Jaleel R., Tanya Milner-McCall, and Tyrone C. Howard. 2020. *No More Teaching Without Positive Relationships*. Portsmouth, NH: Heinemann.

Hyslop, Nancy B., and Bruce Tone. 1989. "Listening: Are We Teaching it, and If So, How?" *The Bulletin of the Association for Business Communication*, 52 (2): 45–6.

Imarisha, Walidah. 2016. *Angels with Dirty Faces: Dreaming Beyond Bars*. Chico, CA: AK Press.

Ito, Mizuko, Sonja Baumer, Matteo Bittanti, danah boyd, Rachel Cody, Becky Herr Stephenson, Heather A. Horst, Patricia G. Lange, Dilan Mahendran, Katynka Z. Martínez, C. J. Pascoe, Dan Perkel, Laura Robinson, Christo Sims, and Lisa Tripp. 2009. *Hanging Out, Messing Around, and Geeking Out: Kids Living and Learning with New Media*. Cambridge, MA: MIT Press.

Jenkins, Henry, Ravi Purushotma, Margaret Weigel, Katie Clinton, and Alice J. Robison. 2009. *Confronting the Challenges of Participatory Culture: Media Education for the 21st Century*. Cambridge, MA: MIT Press.

Johnson, Allan. 2001. *Privilege, Power, and Difference.* Mountain View, CA: Mayfield Publishing.

Johnson, Lamar L., Nathaniel Bryan, and Gloria Boutte. 2019. "Show Us the Love: Revolutionary Teaching in (Un) critical Times." *The Urban Review* 51 (1): 46–64.

Kellner, Douglas. 1995. *Media Culture: Cultural Studies, Identity, and Politics Between the Modern and the Postmodern.* London and New York: Routledge.

Kellner, Douglas, and Jeff Share. 2007. "Critical Media Literacy is not an option." *Learning Inquiry* 1: 59–69.

Kemmis, Stephen, and Robin McTaggert. 1990. *The Action Research Planner.* Geelong, Australia: Deakin University Press.

Kirshner, Ben. 2015. *Youth Activism in an Era of Inequality.* New York: NYU Press.

Ladson-Billings, Gloria. 2009. *The Dreamkeepers: Successful Teachers of African American Children.* San Francisco: Jossey-Bass.

Lanas, Maija, and Michalinos Zembylas. 2015. "Towards a Transformational Political Concept of Love in Critical Education." *Studies in Philosophy and Education* 34 (1): 31–44.

Lee, Carol D. 1995. "A Culturally Based Cognitive Apprenticeship: Teaching African American High School Students Skills in Literary Interpretation." *Reading Research Quarterly* 30 (4): 608–30.

Lee, Clifford, and Elisabeth Soep. 2016. "None but Ourselves Can Free Our Minds: Critical Computational Literacy as a Pedagogy of Resistance." *Equity & Excellence in Education* 49 (4): 480–92.

Macedo, Donaldo, ed. 2019. *Decolonizing Foreign Language Education: The Misteaching of English and Other Colonial Languages.* New York: Routledge.

McIntyre, Alice. 2000. "Constructing Meaning About Violence, School, and Community: Participatory Action Research with Urban Youth." *The Urban Review* 32 (2): 123–154.

McLaren, Peter. 1989. *Life in Schools: An Introduction to Critical Pedagogy in the Foundations of Education*. New York: Paradigm Publishers.

Merriam-Webster. 2020. *Merriam-Webster, Inc.* https://www.merriam-webster.com/dictionary/love.

Mirra, Nicole, Antero Garcia, and Ernest Morrell. 2016. *Doing Youth Participatory Action Research: Transforming Inquiry for Researchers, Educators, and Students*. New York: Routledge.

Mirra, Nicole, Ernest Morrell, and Danielle Filipiak. 2018. "From Digital Consumption to Digital Invention: Toward a New Critical Theory and Practice of Multiliteracies." *Theory into Practice* 57: 12–19.

Moll, Luis, Cathy Amanti, Deborah Neff, and Norma Gonzalez. 1992. "Funds of Knowledge for Teaching: Using a Qualitative Approach to Connect Homes and Classrooms." *Theory into Practice* 31 (2): 132–41.

Morrell, Ernest. 2004. *Becoming Critical Researchers: Literacy and Empowerment for Urban Youth*. New York: Peter Lang.

———. 2006. "Critical Participatory Action Research and the Literacy Achievement of Ethnic Minority Groups." In *55th Annual Yearbook of the National Reading Conference* (vol. 55), 60–78.

———. 2015. "The 2014 NCTE Presidential Address: Powerful English at NCTE Yesterday, Today, and Tomorrow: Toward the Next Movement." *Research in the Teaching of English* 49 (3): 307–27.

Morrell, Ernest, Rudy Duenas, Veronica Garcia, and Jorge Lopez. 2013. *Critical Media Pedagogies: Teaching for Achievement in City Schools*. New York: Teachers College Press.

Morrow, Raymond A., and Carlos A. Torres. 1995. *Social Theory and Education: A Critique of Theories of Social and Cultural Reproduction*. Albany, NY: SUNY Press.

NCTE Task Force on Assessment. 2013. "Formative Assessment that *Truly* Informs Instruction." The National Council of Teachers of English Urbana, IL: NCTE.

New London Group. 1996. "A Pedagogy of Multiliteracies: Designing Social Futures." *Harvard Educational Review* 66 (1): 60–92.

Noguera, Pedro A. 2003. *City Schools and the American Dream: Reclaiming the Promise of Public Education.* New York: Teachers College Press.

Polman, Joseph L. 2012. "Trajectories of Participation and Identification in Learning Communities Involving Disciplinary Practices." In *Design Research on Learning and Thinking in Educational Settings: Enhancing Intellectual Growth and Functioning*, edited by D. Yun Dai, 225–42. New York: Routledge.

Reid Chassiakos, Yolanda, Jenny Radesky, Dimitri Christakis, Megan A. Moreno, and Corinn Cross. 2016. "Children and Adolescents and Digital Media. *Pediatrics.*" 138 (5): e20162593.

Rideout, Victoria, and Michael B. Robb. 2019. *The Common Sense Census: Media Use by Tweens and Teens.* San Francisco: Common Sense Media.

Rubin, Beth C. 2007. "'There's Still Not Justice': Youth Civic Identity Development Amid Distinct School and Community Contexts." *Teachers College Record* 109 (2): 449–81.

Scorza, D'Artagnan, Melanie Bertrand, Melanie Bautista, Ernest Morrell, and Corey Matthews. 2017. "The Dual Pedagogy of YPAR: Teaching Students and Students as Teachers." *Review of Education, Pedagogy, and Cultural Studies* 39 (2): 139–60.

Selener, Daniel. 1997. *Participatory Action Research and Social Change.* Ithaca, NY: Cornell Participatory Action Research Network.

Seltzer, Kate, and Cati V. de los Ríos. 2021. "Understanding Translanguaging in U.S. Literacy Classrooms: Reframing Bi/Multilingualism as the Norm." James R. Squire Office of Policy Research in the English Language Arts. Urbana, IL: National Council of Teachers of English.

Shujaa, Mwalimu J. 1994. *Too Much Schooling, Too Little Education: A Paradox of Black Life in White Societies.* Trenton, NJ: Africa World Press.

Shulman, Lee S. 1987. "Knowledge and Teaching: Foundations of the New Reform." *Harvard Educational Review* 57: 1–22.

Smitherman, Geneva. 1999. *Talkin That Talk: Language, Culture and Education in African America.* New York: Routledge.

Soepp, Elisabeth, and Vivian Chavez. 2010. *Drop That Knowledge: Youth Radio Stories.* Berkeley, CA: University of California Press.

Thoman, Elizabeth, and Tessa Jolls. 2005. "Media Literacy Education: Lessons from the Center for Media Literacy." *Yearbook of the National Society for the Study of Education* 104 (1): 180–205.

Tyack, David, and Larry Cuban. 1995. *Tinkering Toward Utopia: A Century of Public School Reform.* Cambridge, MA: Harvard University Press.

Valenzuela, Angela. 1999. *Subtractive Schooling: U.S.-Mexican Youth and the Politics of Caring.* New York: State University of New York Press.

Vygotsky, Lev S. 1978. *Mind in Society: The Development of Higher Psychological Processes.* Harvard University Press.

Willis, Paul. 1977. *Learning to Labor: How Working Class Kids Get Working Class Jobs.* New York: Columbia University Press.

Woodson, Carter G. 1922. *Miseducation of the Negro.* Trenton, N.J.: Africa World Press. 1990.

Yosso, TJ. 2006. "Whose Culture Has Capital? A Critical Race Theory Discussion of Community Cultural Wealth." *Race, Ethnicity, and Education* 8 (1): 69–91.

Zeicher, Kenneth, and Daniel P. Liston. 1996. *Reflective Teaching: An Introduction.* Mahwah, NJ: Lawrence Erlbaum.